Praise for

Letters to a Bullied Girl

"This book is so compelling because it explores the bullying epidemic from all angles: we hear from the targets, their families, their friends, and, most important, the bullies themselves. At a time when traditional bullying has been compounded by the viral nature of the web, *Letters to a Bullied Girl* strives to show that there's a way to fight this abuse."

—Ann Pleshette Murphy, *Good Morning America* parenting contributor and author of *The 7 Stages of Motherhood: Loving Your Life Without Losing Your Mind*

"*Letters to a Bullied Girl* is a must-read for all young people. Instead of analyzing or proselytizing, it takes us right into the heart of the matter. While bullying is often dismissed by adults as just another form of childish hijinks, it is anything but. It compromises the most basic need of children—the need for security. Our society has tolerated a kind of collective neglect around bullying. It takes a couple of girls who are still teenagers themselves to remind us that every child has the right to feel safe and cared about."

—Madeline Levine, Ph.D., author of *The Price of Privilege: How Parental Pressure and Material Advantage Are Creating a Generation of Disconnected and Unhappy Kids*

"Bullying needs to be stopped in its tracks. A child who is bullied can feel all too alone, and this powerful book can help bolster a wounded sense of self, offer a community of support, and deflect the barbs of cruel, sad cowards. Every child deserves to feel safe in school. *Letters to a Bullied Girl* is not just helpful and heartwarming—it's potentially life-saving."

—Carol Weston, author of *Girltalk: All the Stuff Your Sister Never Told You* and *The Diary of Melanie Martin* and advice columnist at *Girls' Life* magazine

"The numerous letters to Olivia from grown men and women who describe painful situations from the past document how common cruel behavior is—and how long the hurt can last. The good news is that integrity triumphs, and in the end, sisters like the Buders, girls like Olivia, and many others who overcome adversity are the ones who make a positive difference in the world—not the bullies."

—Cheryl Dellasega, author of *Surviving Ophelia* and *Girl Wars*

"This book shows how one girl's life was transformed through the moral courage of others. For all the boys and girls who write to me about being bullied, I want them to read this book to know that they aren't alone, that what's happening to them isn't right, and that they can do something about it. For all the parents who ask me what they can do to help their child, this book will comfort and inspire."

—Rosalind Wiseman, author of *Queen Bees and Wannabes: Helping Your Daughter Survive Cliques, Gossip, Boyfriends & Other Realities of Adolescence*

"As I read Olivia's story and the heroic efforts of Emily and Sarah Buder to help her, I couldn't help but wonder if these same letters could have helped my son Jared, who died by 'bullycide' in 1998. I recommend *Letters to a Bullied Girl* to parents, teens, teachers, health care professionals, law enforcement, and all those who have felt the effects of bullying as a target, bully, or bystander. At some time in our lives, couldn't we all use such letters to help us through our worst moments?"

—Brenda High, founder and codirector of Bully Police USA and author of *Bullycide in America*

"Emily and Sarah Buder are powerful examples of what an incredible impact you can make by speaking up. Suddenly, Olivia Gardner is not alone but surrounded by a sea of voices, many of whom are sharing their own stories of bullying for the very first time. This book is an inspiration and a powerful call to action. It reminds us that whether we have been a target, perpetrator, or witness, we all have a role to play to prevent bullying. We can make a difference."

—Suzanne Shulman, program director of Leave Out ViolencE (LOVE)

About the Authors

OLIVIA GARDNER is a 15-year-old high school student from northern California. She is now forming healthier friendships and is no longer bullied. Sisters EMILY and SARAH BUDER are 18 and 15 years old, respectively, and live in a suburb of San Francisco.

LETTERS TO A **BULLIED** GIRL

NEW YORK • LONDON • TORONTO • SYDNEY

LETTERS TO A BULLIED GIRL

Messages of Healing and Hope

Olivia Gardner with Emily and Sarah Buder

HARPER

To protect the privacy of certain individuals, some names and identifying details have been changed.

HarperCollins books may be purchased for educational, business, or sales promotional use. For information please write: Special Markets Department, HarperCollins Publishers, 10 East 53rd Street, New York, NY 10022.

FIRST EDITION

Designed by Aline Pace and Jamie Kerner

Library of Congress Cataloging-in-Publication Data is available upon request.

ISBN 978-0-06-154462-0

09 10 11 12 OV/RRD 10 9 8 7 6 5 4

This book is dedicated to the memory of Corinne Sides.

A note from Corinne's mother, Rochelle:

The messages sent to the sweet girl Olivia may have very well saved her life. We cannot underestimate the importance of these letters to a current, former or future target of bullying and to the bullies themselves. The isolation felt by the bullied can be overwhelming and emotionally paralyzing. These letters just may be the ray of hope they have been searching for.

My daughter Corinne would have benefited from this book in so many ways. She was a very shy, unassuming child who cherished friendships. After being bullied for months by some of her peers, Corinne committed suicide at age 13. Her father, brothers, and I miss her immensely. She affected every person who met her; she imprinted her quirky sense of humor, infectious laugh and gray-blue eyes on all of our hearts. We are all better people for having known such a loving person for thirteen wonderful years.

I truly believe that if other classmates or children her age had shown her kindness and compassion, she would not have felt so alone and desperate and would still be here today.

CONTENTS

INTRODUCTION

For Olivia Gardner, an epileptic, the bullying began in middle school. It took the form of name-calling after she suffered a seizure in front of her peers. Olivia was singled out as different, rejected by her peers, and tormented in the hallways and on the Internet with an "Olivia's Haters" website created by her classmates. Olivia's bullies dragged her backpack through the mud, taunted her in school, and wore "I Hate Olivia" bracelets. With each incident Olivia withdrew. Wouldn't you?

Olivia considered ending her suffering by taking her own life until one small act of kindness by complete strangers gave her reason to hope again.

In March 2007, sisters Emily and Sarah Buder read about Olivia's story in the local newspaper. They felt her pain and took action. The sisters mobilized a letter-writing campaign called "Olivia's Letters." Emily and Sarah encouraged their peers to write letters to the bullied girl: messages of healing, hope, inspiration, and understanding. Their goal was to let Olivia know that she was not alone and that she had reason to believe in herself again.

As word spread about "Olivia's Letters," the girls' P.O. box started to overflow. Outpourings of stories, support, emotion, and encouragement arrived from complete strangers drawn to Olivia because something in her story touched their hearts.

In these letters, people of all ages and backgrounds share their experiences. Some are young, others are adults who themselves were tormented when they were children. There are also letters from former bullies who reveal years later why they targeted others. This collection of personal memories is the first of its kind ever compiled. The extraordinary honesty in the letters gives us a rare and much-needed look into the life-altering effects of bullying.

From these messages of healing and hope, Olivia was ultimately able to find solace. Today Olivia, who had fled the school environment for the comfort of her own home, is back in school. She has new, caring friends and is forming healthier relationships. Though she'll never forget what happened and is still dealing with the painful memories, Olivia now has reason to hope.

The following pages contain a selection of the more than four thousand letters Olivia received. Though the letters begin "Dear Olivia," they speak to all who have been bullied or who are currently bullies themselves.

Letters to a Bullied Girl exposes the bullying issue with the words of those who know it best. These letters containing real-life examples can help other targets of bullying cope and inspire bullies to change.

This book is only the beginning of what can be a worldwide movement to confront bullying and change the way people treat each other. Through the true stories of the many strangers who reached out to Olivia, *Letters to a Bullied Girl* proves that it is possible for a bully to become a friend and a target of bullying to become an inspiration.

FOREWORD

by Barbara Coloroso,
author of *The Bully, the Bullied, and the Bystander*

Thousands of kids just like Olivia Gardner reach the entrance to their schools every day filled with fear and trepidation, as their bullies await them inside. Some fake illness to avoid school altogether, where they are taunted or attacked in the school yard, hallways, bathrooms, or locker rooms. Others, who reached what they felt was an utterly hopeless and irretrievable point of despair, have turned to suicide, feeling they had no other way out of the pain and torture heaped on them by their tormentors. We hear all too frequently in the news about those whose cries went unheard, whose pain was ignored, and whose oppression went unabated striking back with a vengeance, hurting not only themselves but others along the way in a tragic and final exit.

If we are devastated by the final act of violence, why are we rarely outraged by the events that led to that final act? Young people are bullied relentlessly, and as most of Olivia's letter writers recount, the bullying goes on without substantial objections or adequate interventio
Sisters Emily and Sarah Buder, however, decided to break this si

They were outraged by the bullying of Olivia and refused to become bystanders. Instead they became active witnesses, standing up, speaking out, and encouraging others to do the same. Their letter-writing campaign resulted in thousands of letters offering Olivia support and hope. The news coverage that followed created opportunities for parents, educators, and students to talk openly about the devastating effects of all forms of bullying.

Bullying can no longer be minimized and trivialized, taken lightly, brushed off, or denied. Children, parents, and educators must become more comfortable talking together about what's really going on in our kids' lives. In order to do that, we need a common language and an understanding of the dynamics of bullying—what it is, what it isn't, who the characters are, and how this horrific cycle of intimidation, fear, and violence can be stopped.

Today young people are encountering bullying more than many of us realize or are willing to admit. In a study conducted by the Kaiser Foundation, a U.S. health care philanthropy organization, in conjunction with the Nickelodeon TV Network and Children Now, a youth advocacy group, almost three-quarters of preteens interviewed said that bullying is a regular occurrence at school and that it becomes more pervasive as kids enter high school. According to the National Association of School Psychologists, about one in seven schoolchildren has been either a bully or the target of bullying.

Bullies have long tormented their targets with low-tech verbal, physical, and relational tools; but today they are also using high-tech tools such as the Internet and cell phones to intimidate, threaten, stalk, ridicule, humiliate, taunt, and spread rumors about their targets. Now more than ever we must understand the warning signs of bullying and its various manifestations so that we can put an end to the torment

When I was writing my own book, *The Bully, the Bullied, and the Bystander,* I was startled to find out that many anti-bullying programs have as their foundation nonviolent conflict resolution. But bullying is not about conflict, nor is it about anger. It is about *contempt*—a powerful feeling of dislike toward somebody considered worthless, inferior, or undeserving of respect. Contempt allows a bully to denigrate a peer and feel neither compassion for the target nor shame for harm done.

Many of the letter writers told Olivia that they were targeted about issues of race, gender (including sexual orientation), religion, physical attributes, mental abilities, or economic status. Such bias or prejudice can and will be used by a bully to validate and justify contempt for the targeted child. It is this contempt that fuels all forms of bullying. Contempt comes packaged with three apparent psychological advantages: a sense of entitlement, a liberty to exclude, and an intolerance toward difference. If any of these three are present in a home, a school, or a community, there is fertile soil for bullying.

Those who wrote to Olivia expressed their frustration when others would dismiss their pain as just a phase, a slip of the tongue by their bully, playful teasing, or inadvertent exclusion. But whether premeditated or out of the blue, identifiable or cloaked in the garb of friendship, bullying is in fact a conscious hostile activity that will always include these three elements: *imbalance of power* (the bully can be older, bigger, stronger, more verbally adept, higher up on the social ladder, of a different race, of the opposite sex, or part of a large group of kids banded together to bully); *intent to harm* (the bully means to inflict emotional, psychological, and/or physical pain; expects the action to hurt; and takes pleasure in witnessing the hurt); and *threat of further aggression* (both the bully and the bullied know that the bully has the power to repeatedly target again, and again, and again).

When bullying escalates unabated, a fourth element is added: *terror.* Terror struck in the heart of the targeted child is not only a means to an end; it is an end in itself. Once terror is created, the bully can act without fear of recrimination or retaliation. The bullied child is rendered powerless and unlikely to fight back or tell anyone about the bullying. The bully counts on peers becoming involved by supporting the bullying or at least doing nothing to stop him or her. Thus the cycle of violence begins.

If only someone in the lives of those who wrote to Olivia had been able to identify one of these elements of bullying, maybe the bullying would not have been dismissed as innocent child's play and the target's suffering would have been taken more seriously.

The display of contempt, the use of power, the intent to harm, the threat of further aggression, and the creation of terror manifest themselves in three different types of bullying: verbal, relational, and physical. By understanding the different modes of bullying, we can more effectively address this serious issue.

Verbal bullying is the most common. It accounts for 70 percent of reported bullying. It can stand alone, is often the entrée to the other two, and can be the first step toward more vicious and degrading violence. It is easy to get away with because it can be whispered in the presence of adults and peers without detection. Though quick and painless for the bully, it can be extremely harmful to the target. Younger children who haven't yet developed a strong sense of self are the most susceptible to verbal bullying, though repeated attacks can wear down almost any child regardless of age. If verbal bullying is allowed or condoned, it becomes normalized and the target dehumanized. Once a child has been dehumanized, it becomes easier to attack that child without eliciting the normal compassion from those who are within earshot. When a child becomes the regular butt of jokes, he or she often is excluded from other more prosocial activities; he or she is the last to be chosen and the first to be eliminated. Who wants to play with a "loser"?

Relational bullying is the most difficult to detect and often dismissed as harmless or, worse, as normal. But it is neither harmless, nor normal. Relational bullying is the systematic diminishment of a bullied child's sense of self through ignoring, isolating, excluding, or shunning. It is used to alienate and reject a peer or to purposely ruin friendships. Such bullying can involve subtle gestures such as aggressive stares, rolling of the eyes, sighs, frowns, sneers, snickers, and hostile body language, or locking targeted kids out of Internet chat rooms. Girls use relational bullying more often than boys. Compared with boys, girls tend to play in small, more intimate circles with clearly defined boundaries, making it easier to harm a girl merely by excluding her from a social circle. Shunning (an act of omission) joined with rumor (an act of commission) is a forceful and devastating bullying tool.

Physical bullying is the most visible and therefore the most readily identifiable form of bullying, yet it accounts for less than one-third of the bullying incidents reported by children. It includes, but is not limited to, slapping, hitting, choking, poking, punching, tripping, kicking, biting, pinching, scratching, twisting limbs into painful positions, spitting, and damaging or destroying clothes and property belonging to the targeted child. Boys tend to use physical bullying more often than girls, though bigger girls are known to trip, shove, and poke smaller girls or smaller boys. Physical bullying is rarely the first choice of a bully. If a child has been physically bullied, chances are strong that he or she has been verbally and/or relationally bullied before the physical attack.

All three kinds of bullying can pack a wallop alone but are often combined to create a more powerful attack.

Individual incidents of verbal, relational, and physical bullying can appear trivial or insignificant, nothing to be overly concerned about, or part of the school culture. But it is the contempt, the imbalance of power, the intent to harm, the threat of further aggression, and the creation of an atmosphere of terror that should raise red flags and signal a need for intervention. Sadly, even when markers of bullying are clearly evident—as they were in the bullying of Olivia—we often minimize or dismiss the bullying, underestimate its seriousness, blame the bullied child, and/or heap on additional insult to injury by insisting that the bully and the targeted child "resolve their conflict together" when there is no conflict to resolve.

Bullying truly is a tragedy acted out daily in our homes, schools playgrounds, and streets. Olivia received letters from the three characters acting in this tragedy: the bully, the bullied, and the bystander. While they each play very different roles, they all can become haunted by their involvement and experiences with bullying.

Bullies come in all shapes and sizes. Some are big, some are small, some bright and some not so bright, some attractive and some not so attractive, some popular and some disliked by almost everybody. We cannot identify bullies by how they look, but we can always identify bullies by how they act.

Just like bullies, children who are bullied come in all shapes and sizes. But the one thing all of the letter writers who experienced bullying have in common is that each one was singled out to be the object of scorn and thus the recipient of verbal, relational, or physical aggression merely because he or she was different in some way. Sometimes kids are targeted for no other reason than that they are new to a school.

Differences identified as justification for the attacks are spurious at best, contemptuous excuses at the worst. When a bully feels a need to put someone down in order to feel superior (or to confirm her already superior status), it doesn't take much to find an excuse to target someone. Olivia's seizures were an excuse to target her.

We often look for a reason a child was targeted, something that invited and thus explains the bullying. Yes, a child may be different, perhaps lacking social skills—and yes, these issues must be addressed—but *nothing* justifies treating another person with contempt. Children do not have to like or befriend everyone in their class, but they must honor one another's humanity.

The bystanders are the third group of characters in this tragedy. They are the supporting cast who aid and abet the bully through acts of omission and commission. They can stand idly by or look away. They can actively encourage the bully or join in and become one of a bunch of bullies, or they can be afraid to step in for fear of making it worse for the target or of themselves becoming the next target.

Whatever the choice, there is a price to pay. Actively engaging with bullies or cheering them on causes even more distress to the targeted child, encourages the meanness, and puts bystanders at risk of becoming full-fledged bullies themselves. If they see the bully as a popular, strong, daring role model, bystanders are more likely to imitate the bully. It is not uncommon for boys and girls to use verbal, relational, or physical denigration of the targeted child to elevate their own status in their peer group.

The lack of sanctions coupled with a bounty of prizes such as elevated status among peers, applause, laughter, and approval for the bullying create a toxic environment in which the bully is no longer acting alone; the bystanders have become a bunch of bullies who together denigrate the targeted child further with acts such as creating an "Olivia Haters" page online or wearing plastic bracelets declaring hatred for Olivia. Such cruelty contributes to the cultivation of a worldview that reinforces stereotypes, prejudices, and discrimination. This in turn hinders kids from developing empathy, compassion, and perspective (imagining what it is like to walk in someone else's shoes), three essentials for successful peer relationships.

Standing idly by or ignoring the bully have their own costs. Injustice overlooked or ignored becomes a contagion that infects even those who thought they could turn away. The self-confidence and self-respect of the bystanders are eroded as they wrestle with their fears about getting involved and with the knowledge that to do nothing is to abdicate to the bully their moral responsibility for their targeted peer. All too often these fears and lack of skill can turn to apathy, a potent friend of contempt. Along with Olivia, I am saddened, but not surprised, that none of her peers who targeted her, nor those who looked on or turned away, have come forward with any support, apology, or attempt at reconciliation even after her pain and frustration were publicized.

Being afraid and not knowing how to help are legitimate reasons kids give for not taking a stand against bullying. There are many more poor excuses: "The bully is my friend"; "It's not my problem"; "He's a loser"; "He deserves to be bullied/asked for it/had it coming"; "It will toughen him up"; "I don't want to be snitch"; "It's better to be in the in-group than to defend an outcast"; "It's too big a pain to weigh the pluses and minuses of remaining faithful to the group versus standing up for the targeted kid."

But the cycle of violence can be interrupted when even one person has the moral strength and courage to resist a bully, defend those who are targeted, or give witness to the cruelty in order to get it stopped. Emily and Sarah began a letter-writing campaign that in itself was an act of hope because by doing so, they were saying that there is an alternative to mean and cruel behavior.

Young people are not merely acting out their parts; they are living them. The scripts can be rewritten, new roles created, the plot changed, and the tragic endings scrapped. But the actors can't do it alone. We adults have to get out of our seats. We cannot afford to be a passive, inattentive, bored, alarmed, or deeply saddened audience. We cannot walk out, close the show, and send it somewhere else. We cannot merely banish the bully and mourn the bullied child. It's the roles that must be abandoned, not our children. Our children need a new play, and we adults can become active participants in a total rewrite. This tragedy has had too long a run.

Bullying is challenged when we reach out to targeted young people and let them know that we hear them, we are there for them, we believe them, and that they are not in this alone; when we show them that it is not their fault; when we teach them ways to assertively stand up to the bully; and when we assure them there are adults they can report the bullying to who will hold the bullies and complicit bystanders accountable for their cruelty. Already, through "Olivia's Letters," thousands have reached out to Olivia to do just this, and through this book, they are reaching out to many more.

Now we must continue the legacy of "Olivia's Letters" in our everyday lives. We can build upon the energy and resolve of Emily and Sarah by tackling the cycle of bullying and by bringing it to an end. It might seem like a daunting task, but *Letters to a Bullied Girl* shows us that we can take steps toward achieving it. By railing against such cruelty and inhumanity, we can energize others to be more daring, more resourceful, and more committed to creating more deeply caring communities.

AUTHORS' NOTE

Dear readers,

We often hear adults and other kids say that they think bullying is an expected part of growing up. It is sad that there are people who have become so used to the existence of bullying that they are willing to tolerate and accept it. We think it is hard enough just being a kid—trying to figure out who you are while also feeling the pressures to fit in with your peers. On top of what can already be a trying time, if your personality traits, physical appearance, or medical condition make you appear different from other kids' idea of "normal," you may face ridicule and rejection. Bullying can make a fragile phase of life unbearable.

When we read about Olivia's story in our local newspaper, we were horrified and shocked at how cruel and relentless these bullies were. After reading all the disturbing details of what happened to Olivia and noticing how lonely and depressed she looked in the newspaper photo, we felt compelled to do something to lift her spirits. Even though we had never met her, we felt so sorry about her mistreatment, and we wanted her to know that she did not deserve the cruelty she experienced. We also wanted her to know that she was not alone and that there were kids out there in the world who would be happy to be her friend.

The initial goal of "Olivia's Letters" was for Olivia to receive fifty letters of encouragement and support from students in our high school and neighboring schools, but to our great surprise, the letters starting pouring in and by the end of one month we had over five hundred letters. Teachers from our school joined in and encouraged their students to write letters even using class time or offering them extra credit. When we realized how many people wanted to help Olivia, we contacted principals of other schools and got their cooperation to extend the letter-writing project to their schools. After some media attention, we started receiving letters from people of all ages from around the country and all over the world. The response was overwhelming and the project seemed to take on a life of its own.

We screened every letter and sent them in small doses to Olivia every few days so that she wouldn't feel overwhelmed. It was so heartwarming to see how many people cared about Olivia's pain. They took the time out of their busy lives to write such meaningful letters.

Reading the passionate and revealing letters people have written has been one of the most special aspects of this project. People shared personal stories about their own experiences with bullying, and for many of them it was the first time they had ever told anyone. We feel honored that they decided to share their stories with us.

It was alarming to hear how many kids are subjected to bullying from elementary school all the way through high school. Many adults who were bullied as kids are still feeling the negative impact of bullying on their lives. We had never imagined how widespread the problem of bullying is and how long-lasting the traumatic effects can be.

We are very glad that this project helped to bring the seriousness of bullying into the limelight and has increased public discussion about ways to address the problem. These letters have opened our eyes to the need for school administrators, teachers, parents, and legislators to take some serious steps to protect students. We hope the positive move-

ment this project sparked will continue to grow, leading to the creation of new laws against bullying in schools and on the Internet as well as the establishment of zero-tolerance policies for bullying in schools.

It has also been incredibly rewarding to see the positive impact that all the letters have had on Olivia. The caring and support she received from everyone pulled her out of her depression and gave her hope for the future. The most powerful moment for us came three months into the project when we met and hugged Olivia for the first time and saw her smiling and happy. We have developed a special bond with her, and she has become our friend for life. Knowing she is getting her life back on track is the best outcome we could have ever hoped for.

This experience showed us that small acts of kindness by individuals have the power to make a significant difference in the lives of others.

We hope that the messages in this book comfort anyone who has experienced the painful emotional effects of bullying. We encourage parents, teachers, therapists, and youth program leaders to use this book to stimulate conversations about the need for compassion and empathy.

We personally want to thank everyone who contributed a letter or an email to this project; your individual effort helped to turn Olivia's life around. Please keep in touch!

Sincerely,
Emily and Sarah Buder

Part One
THE BULLIES

"Not a year goes by that I don't feel ashamed."

Dear Olivia,

I have one message that I'd like to pass on to you, and it comes from the perspective of the abuser, not the abused.

I am a 45-year-old, happily married, and well-adjusted man. When I was in middle school and high school, I was particularly mean to a classmate. Ruthlessly mean, in fact. She was from a poorer family, heavier in size, had few friends. An easy target. The torment lasted far too long, probably through my sophomore year of high school.

My behavior plagued me far longer than the four or five years I bullied my classmate. After much introspection, I know why I did it. The details aren't as important as the message: bullies feel better about themselves by picking on others. The bullying has nothing to do with the abused and everything to do with the abusers.

I am ashamed of my behavior, just as your bullies may one day be ashamed of themselves. But I have learned from it. If there is one thing that I would say to my classmate today, it is that I was a weak person then, full of self-loathing and with a black hole in my heart. How sorry I am for not being a strong enough person to see the damage I was causing.

Being abused makes you grow up quickly. You probably understand this already, but please, don't let anyone take away your self-respect and self-confidence.

The good news is that this whole mess is temporary. You'll get through it before you know it.

Good luck with all you do in life,

Steven

Subject: Olivia's Letters

Dear Olivia,

I am glad you are getting so much support. When I was in middle school (many years ago) I was not at all popular, even though just the year before, in sixth grade, I hung out with the "cool" kids. For some reason, when we went into seventh grade, I was no longer cool. I had hardly any friends. And the other kids just ignored me. What I want to tell you is that I did something that I am really, really sorry about now. There were a girl and a boy who people made fun of. I don't think I ever really said anything to them, but in my heart and mind, I made fun of both of them. Somehow I thought it gave me just a little bit of coolness to do that, though of course it didn't at all.

Now I am a minister and I'm also a Buddhist. I've thought a lot about things I have done in my life that I feel badly about, and the way I thought about those two kids is one of the things I feel really badly about. I have apologized to them in my heart, and I hope they have felt my apology in some way. I know you've heard from kids who have been bullied—but I don't know if you've heard from anyone who has done the bullying. I know now why I did it, and I know it may have caused them pain. I hope they grew up to know they are wonderful human beings, just like you are, Olivia. No person is any better than any other person. We are all the same, really. We all have gifts and things we do well, and we all have parts of us we may not be proud of. And we all have hearts that are made to love—it's the very best thing we can do, I think! And everybody can do it. In fact, if everybody did it, what a great world we would have! And you, Olivia, have helped a whole lot of people to learn what it's like to send love to someone we don't even know.

I'm glad to have the opportunity to share my story with you, Olivia, but I'm even more glad that you've found so many people who DO care about using their hearts and minds to love and to support each other. I hope you can soak up all the love, just like sitting in the sunshine on a nice spring day.

Love to you for the rest of your life,

Sara

Dear Olivia,

My daughter is going into middle school this fall, and this story shed light on a situation that is very real and has been around for decades. Your story ripped open an old wound for me.

I was that bully when I was in high school. My "clique" and I said the most awful things to a girl. Later in life, I deeply regretted the words I used to taunt her. It bothered me so deeply that twelve years after I graduated, I sat down and wrote her a long letter.

I told her that I was sorry and that I hoped that my own insecurities when I was in high school did not forever taint her life and that I did not expect her to ever forgive me but that I wanted her to know that I was very sorry.

I never heard back from her, but one day, I ran into her brother, whom I had not seen in many years. He told me that she had received the letter, and it did make a difference to her.

Olivia, I am so sorry for what has happened to you. Bullying needs to stop and I am so so proud of your new friends Emily and Sarah for stepping forward to help stop it. I have raised my three daughters to act the same way as these two sisters. It was hard to tell my children that I was a bully. As a parent I wanted my children to see me as perfect, but I learned how important it is to show my kids that we all have faults and that healing and progressing becomes powerful when we confront our issues.

Olivia, I hope you have an incredibly successful life. Emily and Sarah, I am so proud of you.

Shelle

Dear Olivia,

Hiiii! My name is Lindsey! I'm 10 (turning 11 in July)!

I'm so sorry people were so mean to you. Bullies can be mean but deep down we are all good people. How do I know? Well, I've been a bully once, too. When I was in fifth grade, I hit a boy in the face! I got in BIG trouble and I learned my lesson.

Sometimes I bully myself about my insecurities, but then I have to remember that everyone is beautiful in their own way! And so are you, inside and OUT!

Your friend,

Lindsey

c/o Olivia's Lette

Dear Olivia,

I want to share with you my story . . .

I wasn't the victim, I was the victimizer. I was the one who, unfortunately, enjoyed making fun of and taunting my schoolmates. And I am extremely sorry for what I put people through!!

I have children now, and I have always addressed this situation with them face on!! "You don't make fun of people; it's not nice to treat people badly . . . always treat people the way you would want to be treated." I think my words of wisdom worked well.

I can't help think that if my parents would have talked to me at an early age, maybe I would have never taunted the kids at school.

So, parents, let this be a lesson for you. Teach our potential would-be bullies to be nice, not nasty.

Pam

Dear Olivia,

I have been on both sides of the bully fence. I was a skinny, self-conscious 12-year-old. I hated the way I looked and endured many taunts and lots of comments, which I HATED, about my body! I was a skinny kid, I had asthma, and I wasn't pretty or popular. Somewhere in my self-loathing I turned on another friend and verbally abused her and convinced other friends to taunt her, too. She was a good person, and she and I made amends soon after and we are still close friends. But not a year goes by that I don't think of that and feel ashamed. How could I be so awful??? How could I become the bully that I myself so hated?

I think some bullies are people who don't like themselves. They attack others to make themselves feel better. Maybe those people who are so mean to you are not very happy themselves.

I am 50 now. I still have asthma, and I am still skinny. But I have a wonderful family, lots of friends, lots of hobbies, and I am happy with who I am! And a lot of the girls who targeted me are not nearly as "perfect" as they thought themselves to be wayyyy back there in junior high.

Hang in there, your dreams will be realized, you have some new friendships to nurture, and the day will come when you will know that you are a force to be reckoned with because you survived a trial by fire.

Jessica

Dear Olivia,

Often kids don't seem to realize how much they hurt you. When I was kid I called a neighborhood kid "neckless" because he was built a little different from everybody else. Years later I found out it was a condition he suffered from. He was bedridden most of his adult life and died at an early age. How I wish now that I could take back those words. Someday this WILL be behind you. Hang in there.

Your friend,
Mike

Subject: Olivia's Letters

Dear Olivia,

I saw your story on television this morning, and I felt compelled to join the legions of others who are sending you their support, not only out of concern for you but also because of the terrible guilt I feel for having once been a dreaded bully myself. I, along with several of my friends, made a girl's life utter hell during middle school. I have never spoken about this to anyone because I feel so horrified that I had the capacity to be so mean to someone. It was heartbreaking to see your sad face on TV and hear you talk about your depression as a result of the bullying. I am sure that my actions created similar wounds in this girl. I will always live with the pain of knowing that.

Looking back, I realize how hard it is to be a kid, particularly when you have something about you that is perceived as different. As ashamed as I am to say this, we taunted this girl because we thought she was ugly. Whenever she came into the classroom or out into the playground, a group of us used to bark at her like she was a dog. Sometimes we would howl and pant, but mostly we would bark and everyone around us would laugh. Imagine that! What in the world were we thinking?

It is hard to believe that no teacher or yard monitor during all those years ever heard what we were doing, but somehow no one ever confronted us. The girl we taunted didn't deserve a moment of our torment. I wish someone had educated us about bullying because we were obviously too immature or bent on experimenting with power to realize how we were hurting her.

To make matters worse, this girl's sister was particularly beautiful so people often compared the two of them. She seemed to endure the humiliation all on her own and put her energies into her studies. She eventually went on to become the valedictorian of our high school class; she graduated from an excellent college and is happily married and has several kids. What amazing inner strength she must have to achieve all of that in the face of such adversity. I respect her so much.

I cannot reconcile how I, a smart, caring child who came from a loving family in a close-knit community, could allow myself to bark at someone for their looks. I was not neglected or overindulged by my parents. They modeled values of kindness and respect. If they knew what I had done, I would have been deservedly punished. My bullying was like a horrendous blip on an otherwise normal screen. Today, I am a loving and devoted father to three kids whom I watch like a hawk should they ever be inclined to experiment with power the way I once did.

Olivia, I hope that you are beginning to realize from all the support that you are receiving that you are an amazing, unique person who deserves respect and kindness from others. I commend you for *speaking up* and telling your mother because you not only helped yourself, but you are also helping the bullies realize their mistakes. How I wish someone had told on me.

Believe in yourself,
Stuart

Dear Olivia,

Your story has really brought to light a problem that needs much more attention. As the parent of a bully, I admit to being caught completely off guard when I received a call about my 10-year-old son's bullying behavior at school. The call was from the parent of another child at school. She told me that my son and his friends had been calling her son names and throwing food at him in the cafeteria. She said he "often" wound up with nothing to eat for lunch. I was just horrified and upset. Often? How long had this been going on? Apparently, when the boy asked for his food back, my son and his friends threw it back to him chicken nugget by chicken nugget, grape by grape, with much of it landing on the floor.

I never imagined in a million years that my son would behave in this foolish way. He was a good kid and did not show any signs of this behavior at home. I was aware that bullying is a problem in our school system, but I never thought to ask him about it. Well, I learned a lesson . . . bring up the subject with your children. Let them know you are aware and watching!

My husband came home from work early the day I received the call so the three of us could have a chat about the problem. My son first denied it, but then his face turned red and he started to get upset. He finally spilled the beans and admitted the truth. Olivia, I cannot begin to tell you how hard it was to hear that your child has brought pain to another child. We felt anger, shame, disappointment, disbelief, and confusion toward our own son and sadness for the boy who he taunted.

I am writing because I felt this same sadness for you. I know this was a difficult experience for you to go through, but it can lead to important changes. Olivia, I believe you have a strong will and the capacity to turn the pain you've experienced into positive action.

In our situation, we insisted that the parents and the other boys who were involved be brought in to the principal's office to discuss the situation. None of the boys were able to explain why they bullied this boy. Was it a feeling of power? The ability to get away with something? Group-think? Experimenting with being naughty? What we do know is that it had nothing to do with the boy who was bullied and everything to do with our son's (and his friends') poor judgment. What was illuminating to all of the adults in this meeting was that these kids just seemed ignorant about the concept of bullying, what it consists of and how deeply targets of bullying are affected by it. We all decided that what was sorely needed was ACTION.

Each of the boys went over to the child's home to apologize to him, and they took turns making his lunches for a month. They also formed a committee, supervised by the principal, to find local experts on bullying and invite them to come to the school for assemblies. The teachers reinforced what the kids learned about bullying by asking them to write papers on bullying that were hung in the school hallways for all to read. Posters about tolerance and respect were also put up around the school. A parent volunteer program was started to supervise the students during lunch and recess. The school really took charge and the bullying stopped.

Olivia, my son is very remorseful about being a bully, and I know he will never forget the big lesson he learned from all this. I hope that one day your bullies will get to the same point. I am glad that your message is one of love and not hate. Thanks to you and the Buder sisters for being such strong beacons of light to many others.

Keep up the good work.

Maggie (a former bully's mother)

Dear Olivia,

I am the parent of a 4-year-old girl who has bullied two girls so severely that they left her school. I was surprised that my daughter was the one who was being the bully. I am very sorry for your ordeal, Olivia, but I am taking strides to make sure that my daughter realizes that bullying is not acceptable, before she gets to be a teen. I have realized that this has become an epidemic and people should be more educated.

I was bullied when I was 12, and yes, I hated going to school because of it. Olivia, you are very brave to be speaking out and you have my admiration. I support you 100 percent, and if there is anything I can do, please let me know.

Respectfully yours,
Ronnie

Dear Olivia,

I am a junior in high school and a member of a peer resource group where we support students who have issues at school. My motivation for joining the group was because I have had several experiences throughout school where I witnessed bullying and never did anything about it. Some middle school incidents involved name-calling and put-downs, and in high school, they tend to involve mean-spirited exclusion of people who were once friends. I feel so awful and guilty that I have stood by and watched people get hurt and never came to anyone's defense.

Now I spend many afternoons dealing with the fallout from these kinds of problems, and I don't think people realize how devastating and traumatic these experiences can be. Most kids tend to look the other way like I did to avoid causing trouble of out of fear that their friends will turn against them. I feel very guilty that I never supported or stood up for someone the way these two sisters have. Being a bystander to bullying is almost as bad as doing it, because if you remain quiet, it seems like you support what is going on.

Good luck. Your story has taught a lot of kids the right thing to do.

Zoe

Part Two
THE BULLIED

"As you go through life, you will realize that there are a lot more of us holding you up than them putting you down."

BULLIED FOR LOOKS

"They would look at me and say 'ewww.'"

Dear Olivia,

I, like many others, was bullied in school.

I was taunted about everything. The hair on my arms, the style of clothes I wore, my hairstyles, everything.

Teasing and bullying is never justified, and I believe the reason why I was singled out was because I threatened these insecure people somehow. Maybe they thought I was too outgoing, or too intelligent, or too talented; but that was their problem. It takes a while to realize that, but I hope you do.

Stick with the things that make you happy, and be strong! I would also suggest joining in a team sport in a city league, perhaps tennis or soccer, where you will hopefully gain the support of a group of your peers.

And please share with the other boys and girls who you speak to about your bullying that the most important thing they can do is to talk about the problems they face. As children and teenagers, we need to seek out help from adults and leaders in our lives—but we should also be encouraged to find ways to help ourselves rise above the noise of "haters."

Valerie

Dear Olivia,

I am extremely disturbed to hear what you have been going through. I get bullied though, too. I am 13 years old. I have terrible acne, which I can't help! I have tried tons of medications to exterminate these dumb dots! It's gotten a little better, but I still have it. I get taunted, bullied, and harassed. People act like they're throwing up when they look at me. They constantly throw food at me in the cafeteria. They kick me and trip me. I have gotten into two fights this school year because of other kids. Every day they call me ugly and "pimpleface." They've even said my zits look like spider eggs. Everyday my mother tells me I look very beautiful, but it's so hard to believe because I've gotten "brainwashed" by my peers. I felt like I was the only one, until I heard your story. I feel we have a lot in common, which is fantastic! I'm into karate and I like guitars. I also want to be an actress! What a coincidence!

What helped me at one point was completely ignoring those monsters. If they make a rude comment, don't tell them anything. Act like they didn't say anything. Don't even look them in the eye! That might tell them that they're not getting the attention they want.

I know it's very hard to deal with things like this. Just know that you're not the only one; I'm going through the same thing! I just want you to know that there are people out there who care about you, including me. I hope things get better. I hope I hear from you soon.

Sincerely,
KJ

Dear Olivia,

Hi Olivia, my name is Kyle. I know how you feel. People make fun of me, too. I'm in the fourth grade.

People have bullied me before because I have eczema. They would look at me and say "eew!" Also they call me names and make faces.

Don't let those bullies get to you because I'm sure they have problems, too. And I'm sure your parents love you.

From,

Kyle

Subject: Olivia's Letters

Dearest Olivia,

I was bullied when I was in school, too. I was very overweight and wore thick eyeglasses. When I was in third grade, one boy, who I thought was my friend, pushed me into a big pile of dog manure while others watched and laughed. I felt so horrible that I thought I would die that night. I would leave apology notes for my mother telling her I was so sorry I died and that I loved her so much.

This continued until sixth grade when my parents put me on diet pills (it was the early '70s and this practice was more common), and I lost weight. Guess what? Everyone started being nicer to me, so I thought, "I'll never be fat again." Instead I developed a terrible and secret addiction to bulimia. While I ended up being successful on the outside, I was a mess on the inside. I had a lot of "friends," but none of them close because I didn't want them to find out my secret. I finally went into a recovery program when I was 27 years old and participated in a twelve-step program.

You are young and have the WORLD ahead of you. Know that you are not alone and that you can be anything you want to be and that no one is "better" than you. I bet you have a warm, loving, and forgiving heart. That is something special; not many people have that gift, hold onto it.

And bless the two Buder sisters for their love and compassion, and your mother for raising you to treat others in such a way.

Much love,

Shari

c/o Olivia's Lette

Dear Olivia,

What a brave and beautiful girl you are! I am now a successful registered nurse and artist. However, when I was in junior high school, over thirty years ago, I was tall, awkward, and wore glasses. I was in gym class one day when a classmate, out of the blue, called me "ugly." To this day I remember her face and the way she said it. I was shy for years until I grew up and decided to be the best me I could be, but it took a long time. I hope you will find strength in knowing this is not a new problem, but that others a generation or two before you have gone through it too.

Sylvia

Hi Olivia,

I have told my two young daughters (ages 6 and 9) about how Mommy was taunted very much when she was a little girl about her big buckteeth. I was called everything from "Bucky Beaver" to "Nerdy." As you can probably imagine, I was not popular, and none of the boys liked me. I was lucky that I did have a few good girlfriends, so somehow my esteem didn't plummet as much as it could have.

What made it all the worse was that when I was in fourth grade, I got braces. Now keep in mind that this was in the early 1980s and NO ONE in fourth grade had braces back then. I'm pretty sure I was the first person in the entire school to get braces. So now, instead of being singled out for my buckteeth, I was singled out for my braces! These were not the "cool" see-through or rainbow kinds that are available nowadays. These were the huge and ugly kind of braces that have brackets, wires, hooks. I even had to wear one of those horrible head-gears at night and had ugly marks on my face in the morning from the straps. Definitely NOT attractive. So the name-calling then changed to "Brace-Face," "Metal Mouth," "Tinsel Teeth," "Railroad Tracks," and so on and so forth.

I had to wear these braces for FOUR years to fix my buckteeth. Needless to say, when they came off in eighth grade, I was so happy and relieved. I'll never forget the picture of my sister and me in the front garden of my parents' old house on the day I got them off, and I'm smiling from ear to ear.

I certainly remember the feelings of loneliness, helplessness, and sadness. Because of the taunting I received, I am vigilant in reminding my girls how wrong it is to taunt other people no matter what is different about them. I am proud to say that they have befriended all sorts of individuals, either with or without handicaps or other impediments. I think that it has taught me to accept people for who they are on the inside, and not what they look like on the outside. I also have a husband whom I've known since high school and he loves me unconditionally.

And just remember: the people who teased you are NOT the winners, you are!

Sincerely,
Catherine

Dear Olivia,

I am 72 years old now and I have a hook nose (you can't hide a hook nose, for sure). My brother started the teasing by asking me, "Is that a banana you're eating or is that your nose?"

Then the school kids continued. They called me "beak," "hawk nose," "big nose," and would say:

"If I had your nose full of nickels I would be rich."

"We could turn you over and use your nose as a plow."

"If your nose wasn't so big I could see your face."

"When I see you walking around all I see is a nose walking around."

And it went on for years.

Anyway, you get the point. My learned defense finally was beating them to the punch which cut them off immediately, and it worked.

Letting them know that you already know what they are going to say and beating them to the punch might make them back off.

You are important, loved, and wanted on this earth,

Al—ciao

Subject: Olivia's Letters

Dear Olivia,

You are doing a tremendous and courageous service to many former targets by going public with your sad experience. I'm nearly 62 years old, very happily married now with a great son, but I can still vividly remember the horrible abuse and bullying I received throughout my school years. They taunted me about how skinny I was and how crooked my teeth were. I suffer from recurring bouts of depression (though I'm doing very well right now), and I blame it on the fact that I was conditioned to depression because of the abuse I endured as a child. My parents were wonderful to me, but try as they would, they couldn't take away the deep pain that was inside me, and I bear the emotional scars even today. Kids can be horribly cruel!!

If you'd like to email me, feel free! I wish you the best of luck and much success! Don't let those conscienceless and vicious bullies get to you ever again!

Most sincerely,

Cheryl

Hello Olivia,

I hope your experience receiving letters shows you that you are a beautiful, wonderful young lady. It won't make the jerks and their treatment of you any less wrong, but someday you will find that you don't care so much what mean people think of you. It may not seem that way now, but it does happen.

When I was your age, I was really tall and really skinny. People I thought were my friends turned on me and became vicious and mean even to the point of lying to teachers about me. I thought I was the ugliest girl on earth and felt all alone. It wasn't until I was 17 and started getting attention because of my performances in plays and the band that I stopped thinking suicidal thoughts every single day.

I went on to college and the rest of my life. By the time I grew up, I knew it didn't matter what others said about me. I did find love and a career and a family.

Living well and being happy is the best revenge on those who bully us.

Blessings,
Linda

c/o Olivia's Lette

Dear Olivia,

I saw you on TV, and I know what you went through. I was bullied all through school. I was very small for my age, and I didn't have anyone to take up for me or support me. You're very lucky to have people around you who love you. I know that you will be fine.

Wishing you the very best,

Max

P.S. I finally started growing at age 16, and grew to six feet and 190 pounds.

Dear Olivia,

My 14-year-old son has had the worst year of his life in junior high, but for a different reason from you; he is overweight. Although he is a smart kid, the bullies have made his life such a misery at school that he recently told me that he would like to "exchange his smartness for his fat." One of the girl bullies recently asked my son why he doesn't wear a bra.

In the lunchroom my son told me that each table has an "alpha dog" and that person will decide who is "cool enough" or not to sit at the table. The teachers did nothing about this. When I complained to the principal about it she called the "alpha dog" of my son's table into the office and reprimanded him. The following day the kid in charge took all the other kids sitting at my son's lunch table and moved to another table, leaving my son to sit alone.

Please know that there are thousands and thousands of kids having the same rotten time that you have had and there are thousands of parents, like your mom and I, who would desperately like something done about it. You are so fortunate that Emily and Sarah have come into your life and shown you that there are more decent and good kids in the world than evil bullies.

Good luck and God bless,

Debi

Dear Olivia,

My name is Emma. I am a freshman in high school. I was so sorry to hear about your situation. No one should have to suffer like you did. I think it is horrible that people would make fun of you so much.

Personally, I have never been bullied, but my little sister, Amy, who is 10 years old, has been. This one girl in her class made fun of her because of the way she dressed. Amy was a "tomboy" and wore boys' clothes and skateboarded. She was a unique girl. The repetitive bullying for years made her feel self-conscious. This year, she started dressing in girls' clothes and hasn't picked up a skateboard in ages. It is really sad to see someone's creativity and spirit broken by someone else. Amy became ashamed of herself. Even when she changed her look, the girl still tormented her. It is so sad that the bully wouldn't stop.

As an older sister, I felt really bad for Amy, and tried to give her love and support. I know that the bullying will stay with Amy for the rest of her life.

All the advice I can give you is to try not to let what the bullies say or do affect you, even though it's hard not to. Hopefully you will be able to look back on this as a rough time in life, and not let it weigh you down for the rest of your life.

Just remember, if you are ever feeling down, you have the whole world on your side. When you are sad, talk to a friend or a relative. If you ever need someone to talk to, you can always email me.

I hope you feel better and are able to find inner strength.

Lots of love,
Emma

BULLIED FOR BEING DIFFERENT

"Every kid was more or less the same, but I was decidedly different."

Dear Olivia,

*I just saw your story on the morning television, and I cried. It brought back so many painful memories. I'm a 48-year-old woman who was bullied and abused in high school. I attended a high school made up of mostly very wealthy families, and then there were "the farm kids," the ones whose parents didn't own a beautiful house on the lake, who didn't get trips to Europe or new cars for graduation. I know just how you feel, as I was taunted for being a "farm kid" and my heart breaks for you. You stay strong and remember that one day you will be out of that situation and on to a wonderful life. You're in my thoughts and prayers. *HUGS**

[*Anonymous*]

Subject: Olivia's Letters

Dear Olivia,

I just read your story and I want you to know you are not alone. You said you want to have support from people you know . . . well maybe after this you will know me.

I grew up in the South and was made fun of for being half-Hispanic by non-Hispanics and for being non-Hispanic by Hispanics. I was made fun of for being poor by kids and for where I lived by everyone. I was made fun of for wearing clothes my classmates recognized as having been given away and I was made fun of for being smart. I was made fun of because my father was an alcoholic and my brother had cerebral palsy (and, by the way, he had seizures very often). I had a few playmates but no friends.

Fortunately, when I went to high school, one English teacher saw that I was smart and could write. Next thing I knew I was in honors classes and other kids were for the first time exposed to who I was not how I dressed. Then I got a job and paid for all my own activities and clothes. Soon I was being singled out for my achievements in school as well as for being stylish.

Why do I tell you these things? Because you have the building blocks to take control and prove who you are. You have a supportive mother, you have two young people, Emily and Sarah, who care about you and who have stood up for you.

Where will life take you? Where do you want to go? I participated in as many activities in high school as I was able. I went to competitions for my singing, was a national merit scholar, and as nonathletic as I was I even lettered in football. I even sang with a rock band.

I went to college and became a veterinarian. I have been in almost forty countries. I have been nationally recognized for my achievements and have a wonderful family and friends who know what true friendship means.

Recently I attended a high school reunion and reconnected with a few people who had been supportive. It turns out a lot of my bullies said that they had actually been jealous of me. . . . Imagine!

If I can offer encouragement, please ask me. But believe me when I say things will get far better.

Be strong,
Rick

Dear Olivia,

This is nothing you haven't heard from thousands of others, but I just wanted to tell you to hold your head high and continue on the path you are on. Although your experiences have been awful at best, please know that this time will pass and you will, undoubtedly, rise to heights your detractors never even dreamed of!!!

I was born and raised in a town of six thousand people in rural Iowa. I think I knew I was gay when I was about 4 or 5 years old. Unfortunately for me, so did everyone else! Life for a gay boy in the '70s in small-town Iowa was not a walk in the park, to say the least! I was called every name you can imagine, ostracized, left out of activities unless mothers insisted I be invited, and generally made to feel horrible about my station in life.

Although some continued to call me names, the treatment waned as I got older and everyone split into groups according to extracurricular interests. It may seem clichéd, but I found comfort in activities like drama, band, and working in my parents' clothing store. Not only were these activities that made ME happy, but I found that I could bring pleasure to other people's lives. Before long, I was singing at events around town, being asked to help decorate all of my mother's friends' homes, and looking forward to a life that I knew held a lot of promise, regardless of what others said!

Although I began to feel better about myself, started traveling around the world in an effort to find my place, and embarked on a career in architecture and interior design, I still held onto residual "guilt" about being gay and tried to hide the fact through failed relationships with women and a short-lived marriage. At 27, I finally decided to "come out" to my wife, family, and friends, knowing that it was time to take control. I was convinced it was going to be an awful experience, but didn't hear a negative word from ANYONE! In fact, my grandmother told me, "I always knew, it was just a matter of time." The point of that is to say that anyone who was important loved me for ME. No one else's ill feelings, hatred, or jealousy mattered!

When I travel to Iowa to visit my family now, I'm proud to walk down the streets of my hometown. When I see someone who used to call me names as a child, I simply hold my head higher, exchange pleasantries, and move on knowing that I wouldn't trade places with them for all the rice in China (or all the corn in Iowa, as the case may be!).

Please love yourself in the same way your family and your expanding circle of friends around the world love you! As you go through life, you will realize that there are a lot more of "us" holding you up than "them" putting you down!

Love,
Joshua

Dear Olivia,

When I was a child my family was bullied by people in our neighborhood. They spray painted dirty words on our front window, spat at me and called us names because we were Mexican and didn't have much money and often didn't have food.

One day, a man in the neighborhood came to our house with a paper that he said thirty-six neighbors had signed, demanding that we move out of the neighborhood. I was 6 years old. I think I cried for a year about that.

When I grew up, I became a counselor because I wanted to help people. And my life has been pretty good. There is not one of those bullies I would trade lives with today.

It always hurts, deeply, to be disliked and not be included and not be seen for who you are by the people around you. I know. But those people around you who are bullying you are low-minded and low-spirited. Those people can't like you because they don't like themselves.

You see, Olivia, bullying you gives them a lame reason to feel better about themselves. Isn't that weird that people do that? Because they feel so low inside themselves, they have to find someone, anyone, it doesn't matter who, to drag down, so they can feel up.

But don't give in to them dragging you down. That's not your job. Detach yourself from their craziness, their crazy behavior. If they direct their hate and their craziness toward you, just reject it as not yours and give it back to them. You can even say out loud "I give you back your hate. I give you back your craziness."

And don't forget, they are not really the type of people you will ever want to even associate with once school is over. And you won't have to.

Once you grow up, you will be able to cultivate friendships with good people, people like you, and you won't have to work at getting them to like you because they will see you for who you are, and you will see them for who they are. It might take some time, but when you have one or two or maybe three friends like that, that's all you'll ever want or need.

Hang in there, Olivia. Don't let others define how you feel about you inside. Just look inside yourself and know that you are a good person and that you are doing good in the world. And just say to yourself "That'll do, Olivia." Like the farmer told Babe the pig once Babe had worked so hard and done his best: "That'll do." Take good care of yourself.

Sincerely,

Janet

Dear Olivia,

I was very disheartened to hear about your ordeal and all of the suffering that you had to endure. Unfortunately, as you have no doubt become aware of, this sort of thing has gone on long before the invention of the Internet. When I grew up, I experienced bullying and prejudice when my family moved from San Francisco to the suburbs of the East Bay. I was the smallest in almost every grade and one of the only Asians at school.

The thing is, over the years I realized that kids and adults alike will always find something to pick on and attack, whether it's race, height, weight, religion, money, or poverty. I'm sure you've already heard others tell you this, but it's very true, people often bully others out of their own insecurity and weakness. The easiest way for others to feel better about themselves is to make people like you feel worse about yourself. Don't ever give someone the satisfaction of making you feel bad. You are brave. You are strong. You have the love and support of your mother, your friends, and the people like myself and so many others who were tormented at some point in their lives. Be confident in who you are and know that you are making a difference in speaking out to other kids.

Sincerely,
Curtis

c/o Olivia's Lette

Dear Olivia,

I wanted to let you know that your story is very touching. It brings back some pretty vivid old memories of being taunted for my religion (I'm Jewish) as a school-aged girl in the Bible Belt of the Midwest. Bullying is an amazingly destructive force in our society and kids aren't the only ones who do it. I am constantly amazed to find that adults do it as well. As a family therapist who specializes in working with teens, I see firsthand the terrible impact that behavior has on kids.

It's good to have a support system. Even if you have no idea who every person in that system is, you have their support. And you have my support as well. Stay strong. And good luck next year.

With love,

Margaret

P.S. My older daughter, Emily, starts high school next year. I wish you could be her friend.

Subject: Olivia's Letters

Dear Olivia,

I grew up in Hawaii, and when I was about your age, I had the same problem. I was living in Honolulu at the time and the middle school I was going to had a very bad reputation for bullying. I was the "haole," or white person, in a mostly local population of kids there. I had some local friends, but there was a gang of local girls who took an instant dislike to me only because I was white. They threatened me in gym class and sometimes even followed me when I walked home, staying far enough away that no one would suspect but close enough that I could hear everything they said to me.

There were countless times when I went to the office and said I was sick and wanted to go home early just to avoid them. On the last day of school, which in Hawaii is still known in some schools as "kill haole day," my older brother, who was in college at the time, actually stood in the doorway of my classroom for the last fifteen minutes of school to make sure I got out OK. He had had the same problems when he was in high school, and it only stopped when he grew to six feet tall and became a state wrestling champion.

I wish I had some magic words to say to take away all the pain that has been inflicted on you over the last few years. It's not fair and it's not right that this should happen to anyone. You sound like such an intelligent, talented girl, with dreams and goals. Your victory over all of them is to survive and learn and grow stronger, and reach those goals. You are so incredibly lucky to have found this support, and now you have also become a voice for those who are still too scared to speak out.

I am 46 years old, but still remember those times. I know you have heard this thousands of times already, but you are truly not alone. Those of us who have been through this stand with you.

All my very best wishes to you, and undying thanks to the Buder family for showing that there are angels here on earth.

Elisa

c/o Olivia's Lette

Dear Olivia,

Just want you to know you are a beautiful young lady, and I pray that this letter will find you feeling great about yourself. I know how you were feeling because I grew up on an Indian res-ervation.

And back then people did not want us in their schools. But I thank God every day because I did find a few good friends. But I could never go into there homes or go to any birthday parties.

I now have great friends, so please do not let a few bad kids get you down; they do not feel good about themselves, so they want to make you sad.

I don't know you but I love you and will write you whenever I can, so may God bless and keep you safe from all harm.

Love,
Jackie

Dear Olivia,

I have read about your predicament in the newspaper and also by word of mouth from friends and family. I was moved by your courage and independence and your relentless strength in defending yourself against unjust and unkind treatment.

When I was in elementary school, I went to a small public school in my town which matriculated kids who were all more or less the same. Every kid was Caucasian, came from families of more or less the same socioeconomic background, and had parents with similar beliefs (from parenting to politics). Although I shared those traits with my classmates, I was decidedly different because I am Jewish. In elementary school, because the kids were all so similar, things like religious beliefs were justification for taunting and tormenting.

The worst time of year was the Christmas season, seeing the entire school decked out in red and green and hearing the Christmas assembly sending the religiously infused notes of songs through the hallways. I realize that these kids were obviously immature and sheltered, but it still hurt me that they were so inconsiderate to not even attempt to educate themselves about my culture.

Today I am much more accepted by my friends, and they often come over to my house for Hanukkah celebrations. But more so than the maturation of my friends or my eventual decision to educate my friends about my culture, it was when I gained self-confidence and improved my self-esteem that I became more comfortable with the aspects of my identity that weren't identical to my peers.

I want you to know that I respect and support you wholeheartedly.

Love,

Stephanie

Dear Olivia,

Walking down the halls of my high school isn't the most pleasant experience to encounter. I've been called a faggot several times and recently I was gay bashed during a dance rally and a dance. Considering the fact that I'm gay, my sexuality and flamboyant ways have sometimes attracted narrow-minded and hurtful comments. But that doesn't mean that I have to change. Because I was born this way. At times I have grown tired and weak, almost feeling numb. But I've always thought of the positive things. Both you and I have experienced different things but they've all come down to the misuse of derogatory terms and a feeling of being inferior, the ignorant beings that point out our, so-called "flaws." But if everyone were the same, the world would be boring and uninteresting.

I would be happy to show you around and I would love to be your friend. I could introduce you to new people and I could help you with anything.

Sincerely,
Caitlin

BULLIED FOR HEALTH REASONS

"We all have various challenges in life, but we are not victims."

Hello Olivia,

Probably others have written to you sharing their own stories of being bullied or made fun of. I have mine, too. When I was seven, I lost most of my hearing. I changed schools the next year when I entered third grade. I was struggling to adapt to my deafness (I did use a hearing aid), and the kids at the new school weren't very nice to me. They made fun of me and my deafness and I felt like an outsider most of the time until I transferred to another school at age 10 where there were other hearing-impaired kids. I was much happier there.

I'd like to address what you said, that you weren't comfortable with people seeing you as a victim. I can well understand that because I've experienced the same thing in my life—people assuming that I was a victim because of my hearing and other stuff. Now I just told you a story that seems to put me in the victim mode, but I don't feel I was a victim then, and I don't feel I am now. We are not victims.

Well, Olivia, I hope this helps a bit. I know you said you wish the letters you've been getting were from people you know. Perhaps you could think of us as friends you haven't met or who you are meeting in a different way.

All best wishes to you. Keep smiling!

Sincerely yours,
Jen

Hi Olivia,

My name is Charlotte, and I am in the ninth grade. I heard about your story and about the difficulties you have had to deal with. I can relate to your story a lot. In the fourth grade I had to wear a back brace. I was fine with the fact at that moment, but once I saw what the brace looked like, I began to fret. The first day I had to wear it to school, kids immediately knocked on my back and laughed at me. That is also the time when kids started calling me ugly and the "back brace chick." The taunting wasn't so bad, at least not as bad as it could have gotten, but it still hurt, especially when I had to wear the brace to middle school. The taunting then began to get out of control. Well, my whole point is that taunting is a horrible thing to have to deal with. I understand completely how bad it can be. I pray for you and your family. Good luck with all you do, girl!

Charlotte

Dear Olivia,

I read about your story and when I learned why kids were being mean to you, I understood fully how you must have felt. I was epileptic from ages 5 to 30, and I remember how thoughtless other kids could be.

I always knew that even though I had seizures, I was just as normal as everyone else, but unfortunately they didn't see it that way. I realize now that the reason they didn't was because they didn't know anything about epilepsy and therefore seeing someone have a seizure scared them. When kids are scared, sometimes they respond by attacking rather than by trying to understand. Older people do that sometimes, too.

I hope now that a lot of people know what happened to you and see how unfair it is, teachers at your former school as well as other schools will see how important it is that everyone learn about epilepsy and what it is and what it isn't.

I wish you the best.

Your friend,
Colleen

Dear Olivia,

My name is Stephanie. I am 29 years old, and I also have epilepsy. I first read about you and all the pain you have been through with bullies, on the Internet, and I wanted to write to you because it seems to me that you are a very strong and brave girl. Keep your chin up. People, especially kids, don't always know how to deal with differences, because they are scared by them. I was diagnosed with epilepsy when I was 7 years old and I have always lived with it. It's a scary thing to have. Because of my epilepsy medication I was overweight and taunted about that. However, look how many people have pulled together to support your cause. That's awesome! You can help so many kids who get bullied just like you at other schools! What an accomplishment for such a young person! Keep pushing forward, never give up, and you will accomplish great things! Don't ever believe that your epilepsy will stand in the way of making your dreams come true!

Sincerely,

Stephanie

Subject: Olivia's Letters

Dear Olivia,

I know you wish this support was coming from someone you knew, but trust me when I say I have been in your shoes, and I know how alone you feel.

I am a 32-year-old woman. I grew up going to school in the '80s and early '90s. I was an average-looking girl, on the chubby side. I got good grades and liked to participate in choir and art. I also had (and still have) major health problems and was deeply and visibly hated by most of my classmates.

Although you couldn't tell from looking at me, I have a brittle bone disease and have broken many bones, especially when I was growing up. I broke bones at school regularly and always did poorly in PE classes and sports. I was mocked for my casts on my broken bones, for my crutches, for my limp and my inability to hold a pencil in my broken hand. I was mocked for not wearing popular clothes. I was mocked for having wheezy breath and for having curly hair. Girls said horrible things about me. Kids stole from my locker. Kids destroyed my books and toys. Kids would circle me in the schoolyard and taunt me until I cried. Teachers turned a blind eye or sometimes were even cruel to me, too. I had one friend, but she was not harassed by other kids, and more often than not I felt utterly and completely alone.

You're a pretty young woman, as I see from your picture on the Internet. You are obviously compassionate, and I would guess that you are creative and intelligent. Remember that you have these things—nobody can take them away from you—and down the road when you and your classmates are all adults, you will still have those things, and they will have shameful memories of what they did to you.

Their words and actions are horrible and reprehensible, but you are still you, a human being full of potential and light and love to share; nothing they can do or say will take that away from you. Don't give them any ground; be yourself, and don't be ashamed. That is the biggest defeat you can hand to a bully. They will crush your dignity, and it will hurt. You must shine brighter, be true to yourself, and don't give in. There is an end in sight, I promise you.

In twenty years, you'll be a woman with a career and maybe a relationship and a whole set of friends of your own who you love and who love you unconditionally in return, and you won't give a you-know-what what anyone says about you. You'll look back on these days and remember that they hurt you, but they also made you stronger. They showed you both the worst and the best that your fellow humans are capable of.

Stay strong and true to your heart. Life has so, so much more to offer than the tortures of the schoolyard five days a week.

Hold on and know you are truly loved, know you are not alone even when you believe you absolutely are, and I promise you that getting through it will be worth it.

I know you don't know me, but if you ever feel like you need a big sister, drop me a line anytime.

Love,
Barbara

c/o Olivia's Lette

Dear Olivia,

I just saw your story on the news. I know what you are going through, I also had epilepsy at your age, and I was teased as well. It does get better.

Just keep moving ahead and enjoy the people who are positive in your life. I always feel the negative ones are their own worst enemies, so they don't need me to spend my energy thinking negative thoughts about them.

Good luck, and just know it will get better.

Randy

Dear Olivia,

You are a very mature and brave young woman and I applaud you. Even though this is very hard for you right now, you will never know the impact you have made in someone else's life by sharing your story.

I can relate to your story because I have a daughter who had epilepsy and was bullied by others. She is now 24 and seizure-free, and I thank God every day that she is surrounded by family and friends and even strangers I'll never know about who loved her and supported her and helped her overcome.

Blessings,
Sue

Dear Olivia,

I read the article about the bullying you have received from schoolmates. I would like to share something with you about my little brother.

My brother sustained a terrible injury on his head when he was 4. Several months after the accident, he began experiencing seizures. First at home at night when he was sleeping. But later he had more severe seizures. At that time the school he attended was full of very accepting students and teachers.

They never made fun of him because of what their teachers had taught them: to be tolerant and that some people had disabilities which we should not be afraid of.

When my brother was in high school at a new school, he had a seizure one day in class, and the teacher and classmates all made fun of him and begged the school to take him out of high school because "he scared them." Consequently he was denied a high school education. No one in the school cared and rumors went all around to humiliate him as much as possible. At that time, he had as many as thirty seizures a day

He tried to commit suicide several times because he had so many seizures a day and everyone was picking on him and called him "mentally challenged."

My brother is now almost 60 years old and has been seizure-free for over forty years. He has been married for over twenty years and has held one job for over twenty-five years. He leads a very functional life in spite of his battles, anger, depression, and frustration, but my mother, brothers, and I have always stood by him to help him.

[*Anonymous*]

Dear Olivia,

What fabulous young women you and the Buder sisters are!

I am overwhelmed by your integrity and courage.

Some people may not believe that kids could be that mean, but I do. I have seen it myself.

My son, age 21, has epilepsy and has struggled for acceptance. A lot of people just don't get it, as you know. For some reason, there is a stigma. Sadly, there is a lot of ignorance out there. But I am so proud of him because he just keeps on going, and he accepts EVERYONE.

Thank you for sharing your story. I know your families are very proud.

Thanks,

Carolyn

BULLIED BY GIRLS

"Girl bullies are very adept at appearing polite and reasonable."

Dear Olivia,

I just saw your story in the news and I wanted to write to you. In high school I was bullied mercilessly. I was petite and thin and I had lots of boys who were friends, but the girls hated me. I could never fit in. My family was poor so I often had no lunch, and I had to wear the same few outfits over and over again. I was torn between feeling jealous of the girls who had nice clothes and hating them for making my life miserable. I was scared to step outside of a classroom for fear of being beaten up. I got threatening notes and phone calls all the time.

My mom wasn't much help. She didn't really understand how bad things were for me. There were times when I wanted to die.

Things eventually got better for me. I became good friends with a popular girl who was really, really nice. She was a very good influence on me, and I started studying really hard and I got into honors classes, and from there my reputation as a "smart" kid flourished. The other kids started showing me at least some respect.

My life today is the complete opposite of what it was. I'm successful and I have a wonderful family. When my daughter is old enough to go to school, I will talk with her often about bullying. I'll make sure she understands how awful it is to do that to someone, and if she is bullied, I'll be there to help. Even though it's been more than twenty years since I lived every single day being terrified of going to school, I will never forget how it felt.

My husband has a saying: "Living well is the best revenge." He's right. So study hard, Olivia. Go to college and pursue your dreams, and you'll have the last laugh.

Best of luck to you,
Sarah

c/o Olivia's Lette

Dear Olivia,

I saw your picture in the newspaper; you are a lovely girl. I am 43 years old, and I can remember a time in sixth grade when I was subjected to a few girls who were once my friends who then turned on me. I can tell you that you are not the only teenage girl this happened to and, unfortunately, will not be the last.

Hopefully, you will rise above this and be stronger than they will ever hope to be.

There are lots more good people out there than bad, the bad just seem to have to let everyone know they exist. Hang in there.

Julie

Subject: Olivia's Letters

Hi Olivia,

I have a daughter Yasmeen who is now 11 years old. When Yasmeen was 7 years old we moved from one town to another. Yasmeen was going into the second grade in a new school and with new friends. Yasmeen was very excited and nervous to start school. She wanted to make friends and eventually have playdates since we didn't know anyone in our area.

Sadly, during the second week of school, she started getting bullied by this one girl who was in her class. Though I did not know at the time why she felt this way, Yasmeen would just come home telling me she hated school and wanted to move back to our old home. Yasmeen would have good days and bad days and I just thought it was a stage that little girls go through. But I eventually found out that the reason Yasmeen was having such a hard time was because of this girl who had continued to bully her for almost more than a year by then.

The girl was always commenting on Yasmeen's looks and her clothes. At her new school Yasmeen enjoyed picking out what she would wear each day, because at her old school she had to wear uniforms. But it got to the point where she was having me pick her clothes and triple-checking to make sure they were "normal."

Apparently the girl wanted Yasmeen to dress a certain way or she made fun of her in front of all the other girls and boys.

I was so sad that this was happening and I know it made Yasmeen's life so miserable.

Out of school, Yasmeen was happy and calm. When she had to go back to school she was tense and nervous. We were fortunate that the teachers were very understanding. I guess Yasmeen wasn't the only one being bullied by this girl (most of the girls were too afraid to come forward and admit they were targets of the bully, too).

The school enforced a zero-bullying policy and things did get pretty messy when the bully's mother and I were called to school. I guess the girl's mother didn't think her daughter was capable of such actions. But since other kids spoke out about her daughter, she finally realized that it wasn't Yasmeen's fault, it was her daughter's.

After this the girl did leave Yasmeen alone but Yasmeen would tell me that other kids would make passing comments to her calling her a "snitch" or a "baby." Luckily, Yasmeen ignored them and found really nice new friends.

All these meetings happened toward the end of the school year and due to zoning regulations Yasmeen was moved to another school closer to our new home. Yasmeen was super-excited and never looked back. She made new friends at her school. Some of the kids from her old school wound up at her new school but they left her alone.

It was a tough year for us. I still have mixed emotions about the whole situation and it's not that easy to forget. I know that when Yasmeen relays the story now it's hard for her to talk about it because she says it makes her feel helpless and weak.

Olivia, I usually don't give my feedback on anything but your story was very moving, and I totally can relate to your situation. Bullying is bullying no matter at what level and how extreme. You are a very brave girl and know that you are not seen as a victim. I see you as I see my daughter, as a strong young lady.

Thank you for sharing your story and just know that you have so much support from everyone around you and now from us, too.

Mariela, Yasmeen's mom

Dear Olivia,

I am so sorry you have had to deal with this. We are dealing with it right now with my 11-year-old daughter. She has been picked on for the past two years by one specific girl and several others in between. Last week things escalated as the girl threatened to beat her up and then we found a website she made in my daughter's name ridiculing her. My school has been less than helpful in resolving this. I hope you know it is not your fault. Unfortunately, there are mean people in the world.

I wish you all the success in life.

Love,

Kari

Dear Olivia,

It must be pretty interesting to hear from all these people telling you their personal stories. Well, get ready to add another one to the pile! I know I probably don't have the best official advice, because I've never actually been in your exact position, but I've definitely seen bullying and it isn't pretty.

A while back I became "best friends" with this girl who was very exclusive and definitely a perfectionist. I don't think that I really realized how horrible she was to people, because, after all, she was my "BFF." She would call people "gay" if they did something she didn't like, and would totally tear someone up if they got one point more than her on a quiz. It was truly bizarre. All through seventh grade, I would just take her criticism and ignore the way she bullied people. Mostly, the criticism I got from her was about being "fat." Now I personally wouldn't consider myself at that time as fat, but because of her comments, I got it into my head that I was fat. Even today I am still insecure about my body because of her mean words. This girl in general was just horrible and was not a true friend. I hated being next to her when she would torment others who also hadn't done anything wrong. At the end of eighth grade, I decided that I'd had enough, and I wrote her a very long letter explaining that I couldn't be friends with someone who was so mean. I'm lucky that I got out of it so easily.

I just wanted to let you know that there are other people out there who see through the bullying and the horribleness of middle school and mean people. I realize that your life has probably been changed because of the stupid stuff that people said and did. I know that you are an amazing person who will be able to ignore those fools who decided to make one person's life miserable and get back on your feet and show everyone the strong young woman that you are.

Your experience makes me think of one word: GALVANIZED. It means to stay secure, and stand up for what you believe in, even through the roughest of times, because you know that you'll be stronger in the end.

I hope that this letter brightens your day a little bit! :)

Peace,
Claire

Hey Olivia,

I'm Alison.

I know how you feel. Like you I wish that they would just go away, that you could just start a new life.

I'm 13 years old and I'm getting bullied . . . by girls. They call me "slut," "whore," and "ho" just because I look a lot older for my age. My close friends try to tell me that they are just jealous of me. I think they were bullying you because they are jealous of you, too.

Hang in there and be strong, because when they get older they are going to wish they knew you better.

Alison

Dear Olivia,

I have been bullied for several years by a girl at my local ice-skating rink. She spread some sort of rumors about me, and everyone became very cold toward me, whereas before everyone wanted to talk to me and everyone was very nice. She and her friends collectively bullied me. I actually quit skating for a couple of years because of it. I still have a very hard time going to the rink even though I love to skate—I am scared that I will see her or her friends there and I become anxious the closer I get to the rink.

I know other girls have also been bullied by her or by other girls at the rink, and others who have avoided skating at the rink because of bullying.

D.

Subject: Olivia's Letters

Dear Emily and Sarah's mother,

Please pass on my regards to Olivia and those of my 10-year-old daughter who has also experienced bullying—although far milder than Olivia's case. Your daughters have given Olivia the gift that no one, not even my daughter's good friends gave her—they stood up and said "No." I believe that Sarah and Emily are the real heroines of this story. No matter how vigilant adults are, they are rarely present when girl-bullying occurs and girl bullies are very adept at appearing polite and reasonable in front of adults. The real power to stop a bully, or to counter the effect of a bully, is exactly what your girls did—stand up for the person being targeted, let them know they are not alone.

I believe the approach your daughters took is far more powerful than confronting the bullies because the real damage done by the bullies is that they set off the target's self-doubts and insecurities. If we can help the targeted child to focus on the good things in her life, the bullies are far less effective and may just move on.

Anyway, I just wanted to say, as a mother who continues to be mindful of bullying, that what your girls did is the best solution I have found: other kids, standing up together, as a group, and refusing to be silent bystanders.

All the best to you, I know you must be very proud of your girls. My daughter read about Olivia's story and with tears in her eyes said, "I wish my friends had done this for me."

Anne

Hello Olivia,

Reading your story, I felt that I had to share what happens to bullies after high school. You have so many years ahead of you that these difficult times will matter less and less. I'm 41, and bullies are still around, both male and female.

I've experienced a fair share of bullying from "mean girls" from elementary school to college and even now at work. One girl used to make fun of my clothes and the size of my head! Another girl actually slapped my face.

People like these girls are still in my life, but I have learned to just remain polite, keep my distance, and ignore them. You can't allow people to tear down your self-respect, just realize that you are bigger than what is going on in their websites and their heads. It must be so hard for you to cope, but one day you will be able to look back and see that the world is a lot bigger than school itself.

Focus on your future, your goals, your dreams. I studied psychology, mostly because I was fascinated by human behavior. Despite the circumstances, try to find happiness and enjoy your life right now. I hope you are getting therapy, support and love. Above all, love yourself and who you are.

Best wishes to you in your life beyond this difficult time,

Liza

Hi Olivia,

I was touched when I read your story. I felt bullied many times when I was younger. I remember some girls, whom I thought were my friends, who smashed my lunch when I was asked to play the piano at a dinner for the high school that I was going to attend the following year. Even now, in my forties, I have felt that some of my friends are jealous and critical when something good is happening to me. I have come to realize that they are not my real friends, and I am still learning to weed these people out. It's easier when you're older, that's for sure.

Sometimes young people don't understand what they are doing, and it's easy to want to follow the crowd and be cruel to another person. Good for you that you have a good family to support you. I'll tell you a little more about myself: I was taunted by certain girls in my high school for being a "band nerd," "geek," "wonky," etc. Well, I have spent my adult life working as a professional musician, played for famous people, and been to lots of neat places all over the world. So don't let these "mean kids" get you down. Hang in there and have a good day.

Patricia

Dear Olivia,

My name is Genna, and I have been bullied before. At my old school there was a mean girl named Monica. She would boss me around and she would always make me cry. I told my parents and they told me something that was the right thing to do. That thing was to stand up for myself. Now I hardly ever cry. When I stood up for myself, Monica never bullied me again. I hope you will always be happy and never alone.

Love,

Genna

BULLIED WITH VIOLENCE

"The pain and suffering were etched within me forever."

Dear Olivia:

My heart is heavy for you as I lived through many years of physical and mental bullying during my grade school years. I now am 64 years old, and it seems like only yesterday that two physically big boys singled me out for beatings and everyday pain. One day after several years of infliction, I physically fought one of the boys to a draw, but by that time the pain and suffering was etched within me forever.

One thing it did was allow me to empathize with people who may have had a disability and/or were not as fortunate as myself. It also gave me the knowledge to know how you must feel, Olivia, and, of course, how your parents who love and suffer with you feel. Try and remember that as difficult as it is now, this will pass and you can become stronger in spite of the scars that the bullying may leave.

Robert

Dear Olivia,

I have firsthand experience of what you felt. I never had a *seizure* but I was *bullied*. It was a very horrible experience. I was punched and kicked. I give you all my devotion and energy in reaching your goals.

Sincerely,

Coby

Subject: Olivia's Letters

Hi Olivia!

My name is Bill, I'm a 55-year-old retiree, and your plight has dredged up some really painful memories of mine. I was bullied by a real dweeb from when I was 10 years old until I was about 12 or 13. He was my age, much bigger than I was and a grade behind me. I dreaded every morning when I walked to my bus stop because I knew he'd be there, waiting to pounce on me and humiliate me in his many ways, some of them physically painful, but all of them hurtful to me on the inside. My mom would give her advice, but it wasn't really of much use as I wasn't old enough to understand her. It was so easy for her to say, "Don't let him do that to you, stand up to him!" or some other ridiculous thing like, "Just pop him in the nose!" which would have caused him to stomp me into the ground or something worse; she just didn't understand.

I remember the painful knots my stomach would twist into when I was waiting for my bully every morning, dreading the moment I'd hear his voice, praying he wouldn't notice me. But that never happened, it was a part of his daily routine to target me and inflict whatever nastiness he could while I waited for the bus that never seemed to arrive. I wished I'd had a big brother to keep this horrible person from hurting me, but I didn't. My feelings of helplessness would be worsened by feelings inside that I had somehow failed, failed to defend myself, failed to stand up against this awful kid, never realizing that standing up to him just once would have probably been enough to cause him to leave me alone.

You have no idea just how angry and outraged I and so many like me feel when we hear about this stuff going on and just how much we would love to help you. All we can do is offer our wishes that you somehow get through this as painlessly as possible and do your very best to not allow fear to influence your life. This horrible time will *definitely pass*, though right now, it seems like it won't.

All I can offer you now is the knowledge that you *do* have many, many people who have you in their thoughts and prayers and that this *does* help you on some level. Try your best to keep this from making you a fearful person; when you're older you'll realize there's really not a lot of things or people to be afraid of and that you *do* have the power to either allow fear in or to banish it, it's *your* choice. Yeah, it's hard sometimes and it takes practice, but you *can* do it!

Remember, you'll not only be in my thoughts every day, but also in many others' thoughts, too.

Wishing you well,
Bill

Dear Olivia,

I'm 62 years old, and I was bullied, tormented, and physically assaulted throughout elementary school, junior high, and high school. It was a living hell for me. As a result I became a real loner and I still am. I'm an avoider of people. It breaks my heart to hear about stories like yours and others.

Don't let this get into your head, don't do as I did, don't give bullies the upper hand. Its not you, it's them! You are in my prayers . . .

Dave

Dear Olivia,

Hi, my name is Enrique. I am a fourth grader. I'm 10 years old. Your story in the newspaper touched me.

I understand how you feel. I've been bullied before. I have gotten picked on by some eighth graders. When I was in second grade, the bullies punched me and even threw me. Don't let the bullies get you. Be strong. Your story could help a lot of kids.

From,

Enrique

Dear Olivia,

I am writing with a message of support for you because I, too, have experienced bullying in school.

I am 52 years old. I was bullied when I was in middle school and it is something I have never forgotten. I was singled out by two girls in school who decided to kick me in the shins every day. This was back in the late '60s and girls did not wear pants to school like they do today, so our shins were bare.

These two girls delighted in cornering me in the hallways and kicking me. Every day I would dread seeing them in the hall because I knew what that meant—I was going to be kicked. Other students (and perhaps teachers, too) saw this happening but nobody ever did anything to stop it. My legs were black and blue. This went on for a few months. Every day I would go home and complain to my mom about this bullying. My mom kept telling me to "ignore them" or she would tell me to "turn the other cheek" and try being nice to them. I did try that, but it didn't help.

This period of my school years was so difficult and hurtful that I have never forgotten it. It is a terrible thing to be bullied and that people could even consider treating one another in such a manner is upsetting. Of course, the times are so different and more dangerous now as kids bring weapons to school.

I wish you all the luck, Olivia. My message is to let you know that this same thing has affected others and we know the feelings that come with it. It is a horrible thing to endure.

I am so proud of you for doing something positive with your negative experience and trying to raise awareness about this ter-

rifying problem. I am sure you will make a big difference in this world, Olivia. I wish there were more people with your courage, the courage to step up and make a difference.

Take care.

Sincerely,
Marilyn

To the mother of Emily and Sarah,

As a kid, I was singled out and harassed by a classmate in fourth grade until junior high when it began to catch fire with other students.

In high school, it turned violent and the aggressors began to rouse other kids to pick fistfights with me. I resorted to selective sick days and school nurse visits in order to avoid conflict, and my grades dropped drastically. At the same time that this fairly overt bullying was happening to me, I was trying to keep it a secret from people in other areas of my life at home, church, and in my neighborhood. Obviously, my neighborhood friends eventually became a problem since I went to school with them, too. We silently and unceremoniously simply stopped playing.

Some people will say I should have put my foot down early on, punched back, and saved myself years of grief. And they may be right, but that would not have been me. And I can only wonder who I would have become if I had.

Only as an adult do I look back at that time and wonder why the adults in my life, my parents and teachers, didn't respond to the side effects that resulted from my poor coping mechanisms. Inordinate sick days and poor grades should have been a red flag from a student who had tried as hard as I had in the past.

This is why I'm writing to you, instead of Olivia, Emily, or Sarah. I believe that some adults, teachers in particular, were sufficiently aware of what I was going through and either condoned it or were too afraid to get involved with the politics of children out of fear of conflict with other parents. Others, my parents probably, may have simply responded to my desire to save my pride by hiding and thought it would work itself out. It's only a theory. It was the '70s. "At risk" was not in use, so who knows what people thought back then.

And maybe they were right. There was salvation for me, after all, as older kids in high school didn't know that I was a certified loser among my classmates. They liked me a lot, and I withdrew from my grade level as much as I could without dropping out of school altogether. I began to make friends I previously had not known, and it was they who gave me entrée back into high school society with enough social clout that the bullies largely stayed away. But that was a slow process, one that ended with me quietly ignoring the weak attempt of a friendly gesture by one of my first tormentors. Even then, I was too messed up to recognize an olive branch when I saw one.

The bad news is that I developed a disregard for my educational development and never got over it. I have a bad habit of quietly dropping out when the going gets tough instead of asking for help. Sour grapes should be my middle name because of my quick and keen sense for deciding what I don't really want anyway. And I'm highly judgmental about people who seem to have things handed to them.

I don't accept the authority of people who are simply popular, and it's led me to a philosophy that takes collateral damage of bystanders, misfits, and distant unknown faces into account. Someone we don't even know may be suffering as a result of our actions, so the ends don't justify the means. I don't know that it's true, but I might have turned out to be a much less concerned individual had I not gone through what I went through. I wear cynicism as a badge of pride but realize that it gets in the way if I'm wrong when I question the authenticity of olive branches being offered in life.

I'm making the assumption that you are an adult in Emily and Sarah's lives. And I'm thanking the adult who's allowing, enabling, and encouraging what these girls are doing. Bully awareness is really picking up steam, and everything I hear about this subject amazes me.

Thank YOU for supporting the idea that there is a third option besides hiding or fighting. Public disapproval of school yard bullies should be the unarguable rule, not the amazing and hopeful exception it is today.

George

BULLIED TO THE BRINK

"Don't give up on life. I tried and it is a stupid and terrible thing to do."

Dear Olivia,

I am a parent of a 13 year old girl who was hospitalized in a psychiatric unit this year after a suicide attempt or "bullycide" attempt. Heartbroken, I have seen this beautiful girl go from happy and optimistic to sad, angry, and bitter, with no self-worth, no self-esteem, and no hope. I cry as I write this, not believing that I could let this happen to my girl. I blamed myself for this happening to her. I don't want other parents and children to experience this fate, so what is being done and what can I do to help change this?

Thank you,
A distraught mother

Dear Olivia,

I wanted to write you and tell you that your story is similar to mine. I am constantly bullied at school. I constantly feel worthless. I am also bullied at home by my brothers and sisters, sometimes even by my mother and father. I understand your pain. I want you to know I don't want you to give up on life. I tried and it is a stupid and terrible thing to do. I pray you feel better. I remember I was beaten up by a group of BOYS in middle school, but I got over it. I know how it feels to be bullied. I promise I'll hold strong if you promise to hold strong with me. Your story helped me a lot; thank you very much.

With all the care in the world,

Danielle

Dear Olivia,

I was heartbroken to read your story, as your plight is all too familiar with what my brother went through. You are stronger than you'll ever know. He was bullied and harassed so much over several years that eventually he committed suicide. I found him in his room. He hanged himself. I thought it couldn't get any worse when a week or two after my brother's funeral, I received a couple of prank calls. The callers laughed about his death! People can be heartwrenchingly cruel. Just recounting this still stings.

Much time has passed but I am still picking up the pieces to this day about him. Whatever you do, hang in there, life can be beautiful. Please realize that what you've gone through so far is as bad as it's going to get. In a few short years you'll be out in the world, probably attending college, traveling, forging new memories, all while the trauma you've experienced becomes a distant painful memory, fading from your cerebral rearview mirror. Trust me, I know. I live each day for my brother.

You're in my thoughts.

[Anonymous]

Subject: Olivia's Letters

Dear Olivia,

Take heart, this will pass in your life. How very lucky you are to have had so much support! I wish my daughter had this when she was continually bullied throughout her school years.

She had two best friends turn on her and they influenced others to do the same. It was horrible. My daughter is and always has been a caring and sweet person. Her life was turned upside down. She wanted to kill herself. We put her into private high school hoping her misery would end. But her low self-esteem didn't help her to connect to the right people in her life or do what was in her own best interest.

The good news I want to tell you is that she went for therapy and began believing in herself. She is now, at 27, a very happy person leading a productive life. She went to college, has good friends, and is successful. No longer a target, she feels her own power and can stand up to anyone!

Try to feel pity for those who need to be so hateful. Loving and caring for one another is a precious gift we all deserve.

You deserve to be loved and you are! Just think about all the people out there who care about you.

Sending you love and hope,

Bobbie

c/o Olivia's Lette

Dear Olivia,

I am a mom of four in Pennsylvania and I just read about you online. My daughter, who is 10, comes home every day with such a sad look on her face and she is getting angrier by the week. Your story is an inspiration and I am printing it out for my daughter. She told me yesterday that she is so upset about the kids in her school and what they say to her that she is afraid she is going to hurt herself.

Thank you, Olivia. You are helping more people than you will ever know.

Best,

Cooper

Dear Olivia,

To make a long story short, it started with a game on the playground: "Keep away from Elizabeth." Elizabeth told the teacher, and the girls turned on her. Eight of them chased her down on the playground and hit her. . . . I picked her up from school that day (she said her stomach hurt). It took over a week to get out of her what happened. Well, the girls said they did not do it, of course, and the school did nothing. . . . Over the next three months, Elizabeth started to lose weight. She was vomiting all the time, not sleeping, wetting her bed. You see, the girls played a game on her where they would promise to be her friend next week, and when next week came, they would change this promise to the week after . . . and she believed them. I do not think she made it through one whole school day. I was called almost every day to pick her up early.

Finally, the doctors said we had to pull her out of school. She was dropping weight, and her health was not good. It is still hard for me to believe that this has happened. She is not the same. We have no more playdates. She just plays on the computer or fights with her sister!

We sent her to a new school, and she was doing really well until last week when someone found out and told the whole class about her previous bullies. I lost her again, but I must say when she saw your story last night, she had a gleam in her eyes. It was great to see. We give you our very best. You made one very sad little girl smile again, and for that I am very, very grateful.

Always,

Alacia, Elizabeth's mom

Hello Olivia,

You may think it strange getting a letter from an old person, but my son was bullied all the way through middle school and high school. He became very depressed and even spent time in a hospital because of it. It was only when he got into a supportive college program that he started wanting to live again. Even now he is afraid of school situations and has never been able to get a college degree.

I am so glad you found help and support early so you can get on with your life and even HAVE a life. Now I'm a teacher and I do everything I can to let my students know that bullying is not allowed and it's not healthy for anyone. If I could have spared my son some of his agony, I would have given anything to do so. You are lucky to have a mother like yours. There are many people in the world who do not approve of bullying, and it looks like you've found them. I wish you a wonderful, full life with lots of happiness.

A bullied kid's mom

"The bullies will soon be a distant memory."

Olivia,

Your unfortunate situation has brought to life for me haunting memories and sensations, whose remnants still linger inside of me, some twenty years later. I too experienced wrath and cruelty at the hands of a bully. It started when I was in the seventh grade and only ended when we both graduated from high school. Six years of torment and torture for me—it was by far the most frightening and worst experience ever in my life. Socially and emotionally, it was crippling. I shut myself off almost completely from the rest of the world. My confidence and self-esteem were nonexistent. It was horrible.

But believe me, Olivia, things can work out in the end. They have for me. Surround yourself with people who love and adore you, who will truly appreciate what you can bring to the world. And instead of hating those who bullied you, try to feel pity and sorrow for them. If you can, do not carry that hate and anger with you.

Stay strong, Olivia. Know that there are people out there who are thinking of you and pulling for you.

All the best,

Gerrick

Subject: Olivia's Letters

Dear Olivia,

I first read your story in March and was crestfallen to hear about the punishment you've had to endure from these senseless, hateful people. I wanted to add my voice to the thousands writing to reassure you that not only are you not alone, but you can and will someday have the last laugh if you learn to build your inner strength and ignore those petty, ugly beasts.

Growing up in the South, the child of divorced parents with a New Jersey accent that I had picked up during the year I lived there, I was not a favorite of my classmates. I was a year younger than my classmates, smaller and less prepared for the teenage emotional pressures of school. When it came time for gym class, or for the ride home on the bus, I was an easy target. I was often threatened, thumped on the ear, pushed around, or ridiculed. The kids had a game called "pile on" where the whole bus full of mean children would secretly identify the next victim then simultaneously jump on top of that person, ten or fifteen kids at a time, pushing the target painfully into the seat or the floor. When the bullying wasn't physical, it was psychological, mocking my naiveté with adult innuendo and taunting me with homophobic insults.

The important thing to remember at these times is *who you are*. Nobody can define you if you develop a good sense of yourself—your likes and dislikes, your talents, and your own personality. Give yourself space to be unique and different—the bullies will soon be a distant memory. At the same time, reflect on your experience and use it for something positive. Few people possess true empathy for others, and your experience can be a gift that allows you to understand those who are less fortunate.

By the way, I developed a tactic to defeat "pile on." I was so scrawny I just slipped underneath the bus seat while all fifteen kids exerted themselves to push on top of each other where I had been sitting. Having escaped, I would observe from a distance laughing at their stupidity, a flailing jumble of ignorance. If you ever feel "piled on," don't play the victim, because you're better than any of those people. Someday, maybe like me, I hope you'll go to college, meet the love of your life, buy a house, start a company, travel the world, and live life to the fullest.

Sincerely,
Nathan

Dear Olivia,

My name is Myla. I am an incoming freshman in high school. I read about your story and was touched. I felt compelled to write to you about my own story. I was bullied for years in middle school because I was what the other kids called a "freak." I was chubby and wasn't interested in the so-called cool fads that went around so I was quickly ostracized. I began to have issues concerning my weight and how I looked. It got to the point where I would come home from school and just break down crying for hours. I fell into a hopeless depression, dreading waking up in the morning. However, I found that with the help of a few amazing friends and my wonderful family, I started to see the light again. I am now completely happy with who I am and, although I know there are more trials to come, I look forward to every day when I wake up. I have found that writing of any genre is a great way to express how you are feeling.

You just have to remember that there are the people out there who will tell you that you're not good enough, but there are so many more people who are right beside you pushing you to achieve your dreams. Those people will remind you that you are beautiful inside and out. I hope that you continue to draw strength from these letters. You are a role model to those who have been bullied everywhere.

Sincerely,
Myla

c/o Olivia's Lette

Dear Olivia,

I was also a target of bullying from elementary school through high school. It really did affect my life. I have had a hard time trusting people and making friends due to my experiences. Now that I am 35 with a 15-month-old son, I've decided that I can't go through life using my bullying experience from my childhood as an excuse to keep me isolated from relationships. I admire your courage and pray that your letter-writing campaign and media publicity will give others hope and strength.

Much admiration,

Leigh

Dear Olivia,

I was not so lucky socially, especially from sixth to eighth grade. I remember being taunted mercilessly by the "cool" kids, who found me very uncool, a "goody two-shoes," and not willing to engage in all the risk-taking behaviors that many adolescents start experimenting with. I was probably just a big nerd who cared about getting good grades and didn't know how to fit in. I remember being reduced to tears and running to the bathroom on more than one occasion. I remember asking for my entire schedule to be changed so I wouldn't have to see one particular mean girl. I remember trembling before I had to enter the classes where the kids were particularly brutal to me. It's still a very painful time in my life for me to look back on.

At the age of 47, however, I can say that I weathered that time, that kids grow up and mature and don't necessarily stay as mean, that I have many close friendships, a supportive family, and a loving husband.

So, Olivia, I completely empathize with what you have gone through. Hold onto the people in your life who love you and know that people do have the capacity to get nicer when they mature. I'm glad these letters show you how many good and compassionate people there are in this world.

Thinking of you,
Paula

Hello Olivia,

I have read about all the horrible abuse you have had to go through at the hands of your classmates. I understand what you are going through. When I was in high school all my classmates turned on me, I was laughed at in the halls, made fun of online, people even printed permanent messages in my senior class yearbook. I felt so alone, so horrible and I just wanted to get away. I am 20 years old now and am a new person. Trust me, you can get through this, you will get through this. I cannot say it isn't difficult, because it is. But know that your family loves you, and you have the support from thousands of people who have been in your situation and know it can change. Stay strong, you will make it through.

Mollie

Subject: Olivia's Letters

Dear Olivia,

In elementary school I was smart, but very skinny and not physically strong so I got picked on at times. In middle school I got picked on even more. I wasn't part of the in crowd, and because I was a "nice" boy, I was taunted and picked on. At one point I tried to defend myself and someone hit me in the head from behind with a combination lock. But as bad as those times were it was nothing like my first year in high school. I didn't go to the neighborhood high school, and I would ride the bus staring out the window dreading the ride to school, eagerly waiting to go home. I wasn't really bullied or picked on at high school, but I was shunned, I didn't fit in, I was isolated. It got to the point where I couldn't bear to go to school, so I would skip class and go to the movies. The school was going to kick me out, I failed almost every class. But my mom stood up for me, she said if they gave me a chance I could succeed, so they put me on probation. I couldn't do anything about the bus ride to school, but I started taking an alternate route home and I replaced skipping school and going to the movies with going to the public library after school. I read tons of books. My grades were good, but one turning point for me was when I got an F on a paper I wrote because my English teacher said I could do better. My teacher, Mrs. Page, believed in me, and when my mom came to school, Mrs. Page told my mom how much talent I had. I wrote a short story and read it before the class, and everyone applauded (just like in the movies!). Eventually I did make some friends, and things worked out in the end for me (so remember you are not alone, there is always hope).

Zandy

Hi Olivia,

My wife was six feet tall and weighed ninety-nine pounds when she was 13 years old. Her schoolmates taunted her all the time, calling her "Olive Oyl" (the name of Popeye's girlfriend) because she was so tall and skinny. She went on to be a model, and we have been very happily married for thirty-eight years.

Hang in there. Don't let 'em get you down. Life can unfold in wonderful, mysterious ways. Be strong.

David

c/o Olivia's Lette

Dear Olivia,

When I was young, I was picked on every day. People said that I was weird, that I looked funny, that I acted funny. People threw my back-pack in the mud, too. When I became older, I became successful—I got the career I wanted, and I kept the friends in my life that I liked.

If I was at your school, I would have stood beside you as others picked on you.

Just keep being a good person, life will find a way to hold your hand—and you will keep the friends who are worth keeping.

Aditya

Olivia,

My heart goes out to you and to everyone who is or has been bullied. I have been there.

I have a speech impediment and throughout school I was taunted and bullied. Students made me feel like I was subhuman, mentally retarded and rejected by society. I felt alone, so totally alone. My only comfort was my pet dog which gave me unconditional love.

I remained passive even when I was verbally and physically attacked by classmates. My friends would not come to my defense due to peer pressure. Many times I would go home crying. I hated school! My parents thought that this problem was trivial and usually placed the blame on me. Did this leave an emotional scar on my life? Yes, it did. . . . Let me explain.

I am a 54-year-old male working as an information technology professional. Reflecting on my past experiences helped to mold what I am today. The viciousness and cruelty of classmates made me realize that I never wanted to be like them. I learned compassion and empathy for everything living. I am not a religious person, but I truly believe in the golden rule (treat others as you would like to be treated) which was reinforced as the result of being humiliated by classmates.

After graduating from college with a degree in engineering I started my professional career. Working in the corporate world sometimes can be rough. Many employee personalities come into play in the business world, some of which can be cruel. But one of my goals, or I should say philosophies, is to touch each and everyone I cross in a positive manner. I gain a personal sense of pleasure in going out of my way to be kind to everyone, even to strangers and impolite people. Sometimes this isn't easy. Some people say they must earn their respect, but I say that I respect everyone until proven otherwise.

Life is very precious and is far too short to hold hostility or a grudge against people. With age comes wisdom and you will see as you grow older that your classmates were too immature to understand the ramifications of their brutality. While attending several of my high school reunions many of my classmates came up and apologized for their actions. Several stated that they couldn't understand why they did what they did, but later understood that their actions were harmful.

The bottom line is life is incredibly precious and you must live it to its fullest extent with joy and harmony. Only then can you better yourself.

Sincerely,
Nick

Subject: Olivia's Letters

Dear Olivia,

I, too, was bullied as a child. Fourth, fifth, and sixth grades were the worst for me—the boys would shove me down on the playground, the girls called me names and did things like tear up my homework and trip me in the halls. I hated them, and school, with every fiber of my being. I never did anything to provoke this treatment—it was not my fault, even though I felt that way when I was at my worst. There were times I thought of killing myself, but I could never bring myself to do it, and I'm glad of that now.

My parents helped me turn things around. They believed in me no matter what, and gave me the strength to pick up and keep going, no matter how many times I was knocked down. In junior high, I made a good friend and was not so isolated, and by the time I was in high school, I had been elected vice president of my class and had many friends. To this day, I am filled with anger when I see or hear of bullying. No person, man or woman, adult or child, should have to be subjected to it. I live my life doing everything I can to stop it when I see it—in the workplace, in my children's schools, everywhere.

The important thing for you to remember is that there is an end to it. You've got a lot of strength in you, and sooner or later, you will get the sweetest revenge of all on the bullies—a life well-lived, a strong character and a deep personal understanding of the value of friendship.

Never give up. Never let them win. You've got people the world over on your side now, you'll never be alone in this fight.

Be strong,

Adam

Dear Olivia,

I would like to congratulate you on your poise and maturity for a girl your age. I thought I would write to you and tell you about my two daughters. One is 24, and the other is 21. When the older one was in middle school she wore glasses and braces and she did not feel good about herself. But she would not let anyone destroy her spirit. She learned to stick up for herself. And she learned not to care about what other girls said about her. She really became a little mighty might! By high school she made the cheerleading squad and also was elected captain in her senior year. She went onto college and was also elected president of her sorority. If I showed you a picture of her in seventh grade, you would not believe she was the same girl.

The younger one is in her junior year of college and just switched colleges because there was a group of girls that was making her life miserable. I am so happy that she is now at home and commutes to a closer college. She was just tired of the "girl drama" she had to deal with at her previous college. She has always had problems with girls because she is so pretty and all the guys want to date her. My daughters have grown to feel secure about themselves and for that I am most grateful.

Well, I just wanted to tell you to stand tall and keep your chin up! You will end up having a happy life. Keep a smile on your face and happiness will flow your way! You don't have to write back because I know you already have a lot of letters you want to answer. I'm cheering for you!

Deb

c/o Olivia's Lette

Dear Olivia,

I was bullied when I was your age, and I turned out just fine. Hang in there!!! I am praying for you.

Cynthia

Dear Olivia,

Your story broke my heart. When I was in seventh grade, my entire group of friends turned on me overnight. Suddenly, I had no friends. I could not ride the bus or walk to school or I would literally get beaten up by a huge group of girls. I also had to leave campus during lunch. My school basically shrugged their shoulders and said it was just kids being kids. I lived in fear for three years until we moved to a different state.

This affected me for much longer. I turned right around and bullied my younger sister. My self-esteem was shattered and I also engaged in a lot of destructive behavior and I had trouble trusting female friends.

So the story gets better—as an adult, I have a great career, a great marriage, two small children, and a large group of close friends. I graduated with high honors from a top university. I'm probably doing better than 99 percent of my junior high peers but that's not important to me anymore. I can't even remember some of their names. As a parent, I am making sure my children treat others with care and respect.

I wish someone would have told me this: these years are a very short period of your life. You will barely remember the people who are currently making your life hell. The jerks who are torturing you will go on to be the kind of people who others do not trust or want to hire. They will have fake friends and screw each other over for most of their lives. However, these experiences will help give you empathy for others and the ability to sort the good people from the bad.

Don't give people who treat you poorly any of your attention or energy because they don't deserve it—save yourself for the people who are good to you.

Hang in there. Give yourself time to work through this because it will take you time to get over it, and be kind to yourself. Although it's tough now, this is a tiny part of your life.

Focus on your dreams.

[Anonymous]

Dear Olivia,

Thank you for being so brave as to put your story out for the world to know. By doing this, you are helping to bring an end to this soul-wrenching torture that so many of us have endured over the years. You are no longer a target, but instead have become an advocate and a champion for those who want to rise above their bullies. The two sisters who stepped in on your behalf are examples of the closest things we have to angels in this world.

I am writing with tears as I remember (I am now 52) my years of isolation and hiding from classmates and even one teacher. I tend to put out of my mind those years until I read stories like yours.

My bullying nightmare started because my father was a scout leader in my school. He ran the troop like it was a Marine Corps boot camp. Many of the scouts were the older brothers of my classmates. The scouts, not being able to retaliate directly against my father, instead turned their younger brothers to attack me starting in third grade through high school. One teacher, who I deeply admired, even conjugated the word ugly using me as an example for the superlative, ugliest. The class roared with approval. For years I was always ashamed to show my "ugliest" face to anyone and years later rarely dated. As a result I changed from a regular outgoing kid to one who learned that people were mean and to be avoided. So I avoided people as much as possible. It wasn't that I disliked people, I just felt I was so wretched that it was better to not inflict myself on others.

It was a few years after high school that I began to see that bullies were truly tiny-minded cowards, something I actually was not. I also began to make friends with caring, emotionally mature people and gradually came to believe that the vast majority of people won't tolerate bullies, especially as the awareness of this all too common horror continues to grow. The Internet has tremendous power!

My experience has helped to make me a compassionate, understanding human being. As the expression goes: "What doesn't kill us makes us stronger." I've also found this to be true.

You are really fortunate to have been able to see how many people care about you in a huge way.

Best regards,
Jack

Dear Olivia,

I do so know what you've gone through. I was picked on to no bitter end all through school. I was this tiny little kid and of course a complete target for big bullies. I wanted to just die and go away. It all got so bad after so many years of it. Well, I'm glad I hung in there because I'm the president of my own computer services company and I have a great life. There are millions of us on your side and we're all out here to help you if you need it.

Lucas

c/o Olivia's Lette

Olivia,

I too was bullied in school. But I graduated, then promised myself to NEVER be like my bullies. I can't say my life has been perfect, but I can say that I kept my promise.

I am not like them and neither are you.

Please do not let these people get you down. Life is just too short. Go out and have fun, enjoy this time.

I won't forget you. I promise to pray every time you cross my mind, that you will have a wonderful, FUN day.

Hearts,

Elizabeth

Dear Olivia,

My name is Clare, and I am a sophomore in high school. And I would like to tell you a story about my experiences with some pretty nasty bullies. It happened in seventh grade when I was 12 years old. There was a new girl in my grade named Madison who everyone automatically liked. I liked her, too, until my best friend decided she liked Madison better. So I was jealous and hurt because my best friend could never hang out anymore and I was left friendless. Soon things got worse. They wouldn't even let me sit at the same table as them for lunch, and when Madison and I were assigned to be partners on a project, she made gagging noises to the classroom. I felt like I couldn't go to anyone to talk about this, not my mom, sisters, teachers. I thought they would make it worse. Not only were my friends detaching themselves from me, I was detaching myself from the world.

Then on April 15 (I still remember this day forever), our music teacher was absent and we had a sub. He was a guy named Jake who was in a band and wanted us kids to try to play his instruments. He picked me out first to play the guitar, and as you can imagine I was horrified. "Don't mess up, Clare," Madison snickered as the rest of the class giggled. "Now it's not too easy, try just these simple chords," Jake told me, ignoring the class. And you know what happened? I was really good! Well, not amazing, but for a first-time player, I was really good. Playing the guitar gave me confidence and gave me an outlet for my creativity.

I formed a band with a few other girls, and we won the

school talent show at the end of the year! Afterward my best friend tried to come up to me and congratulate me, and I did give her a hug. "I'm sorry about this year, Clare," she said sadly. "Things got out of control." My ex-best friend and I are now friends again, for we both have matured, and things are going very well.

Things might seem awfully tough right now, but there is always the future to look forward to. Are the kids at school not mature enough now? They will be one day. My best advice for dealing with bullies? Just remember that they are probably not secure enough in themselves so they have to make other people feel bad. They are so LAME! I wish you the best of luck with all your future endeavors!!!

Clare

Subject: Olivia's Letters

Olivia,

I am so sorry that you have been so badly treated by your schoolmates. I am so proud of you though, for standing up and letting people know about what happened to you because only by shining a light on the horrible behavior will it end. I know. Many, many years ago when I was in my sophomore year of high school, I witnessed one of my classmates shoplift a jacket when we were out on a school-sponsored activity. Thinking back now, she was not very smart as she had on a sweatshirt with the name of our high school written across her chest when she was committing the crime. I did not know what to do and headed back to school.

She and the other people who shoplifted caught up with me and threatened me not to tell anyone. When my mom picked me up from school, she knew something was wrong right away, and I had to tell her. She and my dad were very disappointed in me that I had not said something in the shop when the stealing occurred and then insisted that I tell the principal of my school the next day. I refused because I knew what the consequences would be and begged my parents not to say anything. We finally reached a compromise that my parents would go in to tell the school what happened and in order to protect me, we would ask that I be punished along with the rest of the people involved so it would not look like I "snitched." Despite my parents' best efforts (and my suffering through the punishment with the others!), word got out that I was the narc.

For three long years, I was tormented—mainly by the "in" crowd who were all the athletes. I had actually been an athlete until this happened and then did not want to play sports anymore because of how I was treated. People would whisper "narc" under their breath in class and they would say it in the halls as I walked past. I sadly thought that after the summer and when my junior year began, they would actually find someone else to pick on; they did not. My parents wanted to complain to the school, but I would not let them, as I pointed out to them what happened when they went to the school the first time. Teachers were aware of what was going on but ignored it because the people who were bullying me were popular athletes.

During my senior year (three years after the incident and the shoplifter had been expelled from the school for some other infraction), some people tried to run me off the road on the way to school yelling "narc" as they drove by.

At a football game, one of the sons of a prominent teacher on campus poured soda and popcorn over me calling me a snitch. With two weeks left to go in the school year, my parents had had it and went in to complain. The prominent teacher was upset that my parents had complained about his son and demanded to know from me how I could accuse his son of such things!

In the end, I graduated and went to a fabulous college where I learned that my experience was not unusual. As a matter of fact, at a wedding with some other friends from high school, I found out that other people had been bullied by the same people I was. One girl even had the inside of her convertible covered with human feces. We had all suffered in silence.

I am now a successful lawyer in San Francisco (or so I like to think!). You will survive this. It is horrible and painful to go through and while I would never wish it on anyone, I think that the experience helped to make me a more compassionate person. I am much more sensitive to other people and am always trying to look out for others who I feel may be treated badly. I stand up for myself now and for others. That was my mistake, being silent and hoping that the bullies would move on to someone else. I have a set of 17-month-old twins and I will raise them to stand up for themselves and to never make fun of or bully another person.

Keep your chin up, Olivia, and be proud of who you are. Never let anyone ever make you feel less of a person than you obviously are. Also be grateful that your mom is so supportive and loves you so much. I am sure (now that I am a mom) that your hurt has pained her almost as much as, if not more than, it has pained you.

Good luck,

Jeanine

Dear Olivia,

I'm 68, and my brother is 66. We grew up on the north shore of Long Island in the 1950s when polio hit. Several children in our town who got it weren't very lucky. Some were affected physically. My brother was friendly with Bill, one of those physically affected, and he and another guy named Peter hung out with him in high school. Most other classmates stayed away from him, as they didn't want to be friends with a "gimpy" who limped. Thirty some years later, my brother got a call from Bill. He said he thought about the two of them over the years, and was glad to locate them, as he always was grateful for their friendship, because others shunned him. My brother said that he never considered anything but what a nice person Bill was, and that's all that mattered.

There's a great follow-up to this. My brother and I have always been interested in cars, and I subscribe to several magazines. Several months after my brother received the call from Bill, I was looking at an article about someone in southern California who has an extensive collection of classic Corvettes. There was a picture of some of the cars in front of a very impressive house, and the name of the owner was the same as my brother's friend Bill. My brother called him up and asked if he was the same person mentioned in the article. He said he was, and that he got into the Internet business very early and was extremely successful in it. My brother asked him why he didn't mention it during their conversation, and he replied that it wasn't important, but that their friendship in high school was.

Sincerely,

Tony

For Olivia,

Please accept this note of support. I had no idea such things could happen to girls. I have a 4-year-old of my own, and I was bullied all the way through college. But the good news is that you won't be. I'm very proud of your mom and the two sisters who took a stand for your life. Knowing what it's like to be bullied has had a profound effect on my life—even to this day. I always wondered "why me?" probably just like thousands of other kids. Now with the advent of the Internet, the bullies are "always on." At least back when I was a boy, I could hide a little bit easier.

Please know that you are not alone. I still bear the scars, and you know what? I bear them with dignity because I know I've been through the worst humanity has to offer and found myself prospering outside of school. I found that the bullies faded away like nightmares once I started working and finding my identity, friends I could trust, and a wonderful wife. But I will never forget my bullies, and sometimes I wish I could ask them, at this age, "why?"

But I know whatever answer they give will ring hollow. There is no answer or excuse. Just know that you have already surpassed what any bully can do to you by reaching out to others.

You're a champion. I wish you all the best life has to offer. Just remember how brave you are and that you can do anything.

Stay close to those letters of support. Each person's words represent someone just like you who is also willing to stick up for you and support you. Believe in yourself. You have already proven your resiliency. I don't think there is much more that I can say except "have a wonderful life." You deserve every bit of it!

Jim

c/o Olivia's Lette

Dear Olivia,

I just wanted to let you know that I was bullied when I was your age. I thought that I would never survive it. I turned to my artwork to express my feelings at the time.

I completely understand how horrible it makes you feel about yourself. Well, now I'm 41 (I can't believe how old I am!) and I love my life. It takes some time, you have to be strong, but I know everything is going to turn out just fine.

Take care,

Peter

Subject: Olivia's Letters

Dear Olivia,

My name is Dana. I am much older than you are, but I wanted to write to you to give you some encouragement and tell you my own story.

I was bullied in school, too. I guess it was at its worst in middle school. At the time, I felt really terrible about it. I just wanted to fit in and be like the other kids, so I would be liked by them. It seemed like no matter what I did, I was always ridiculed. After awhile, I guess in high school, I just quit trying to fit in, but and it was also at this time that I started to figure out something.

My husband and I talk about this topic all the time. "Normal people" can sense something about you that is different, and it bothers them without quite knowing or understanding why. This difference could be talent, beauty, creativity, it is a special spark about you that sets you apart from the rest. I realized when I grew up that there were others like me. These people were always very intelligent, had a unique way of looking at the world, and were highly creative—artists, musicians, writers.

While it may not seem like it now, you will also learn that by going through these emotional and hurtful times, you will become a more sensitive and empathetic person. You will have an insight into human psychology that these other people are incapable of attaining. You will be able to understand and "read" people better than the average person.

I know it's awful to go through. Sometimes I didn't think I would make it through the day. I hated going to school, and I would avoid everyone. But it will get better. In the meantime, cultivate your mind, become the best person you can be. Read all you can, especially biographies about interesting people who were persecuted for their uniqueness; your parents or librarian should be able to help you out here. Fiction is also a big help. It will take you away to another time and another world. Rest assured that you are a good and great person who is just ready to blossom into the world. Someday you'll be happy that you were the unique and special child that you were. You certainly don't want to live an average humdrum life, do you? And I can see that you aren't!

Good luck and all the best to you. You are a beautiful and special girl.

With warmest wishes and a big hug!

Love,
Dana

Dear Olivia,

My heart goes out to you, and I really do know exactly how you feel. I am 53 years old, and from fourth through sixth grades I was bullied. I was kicked, punched, called names, ostracized, always the last one to be chosen for anything ("ewwww, we don't want her on our team!"), my lunch and personal items were ruined, and I dreaded every school day with every ounce of my being. Kids are bullied for a thousand reasons, none of them valid. I want to tell you that even though you will always remember the things that have happened to you, you will feel better about them and not let them rule your life. It will pass, even though it doesn't feel like it right now, and it will hopefully help shape you into a better, kinder, and more understanding person. Do not give the bullies the satisfaction of turning you into a mean and spiteful person; at some point, some of them will regret the way they treated you.

Good luck to you. Hold your head up and know that you are the one who is right.

Blessings to you,
Caren

Part Three
HEALING WORDS

"You will contribute beautiful gifts to this world because you know the inherent and infinite value of every human soul."

Dear Olivia,

My heart reaches out to you so fervently as I imagine what must have been a heartbreaking ordeal for you to go through. And yet, even as I empathize with your suffering, I feel very strongly that you are going to emerge a very fierce, centered, relevant woman, achieving successes greater than what seems possible at this time, borne out of the senseless psychological violence you have endured.

I have had to bear many injustices and slights over my lifetime, as well as tremendously hurtful assaults on my spirit, such as those to which you have been repeatedly subjected. While these trials felt permanently damaging at the time, I can truthfully tell you this: You will contribute beautiful gifts to this world because you know the inherent and infinite value of every human soul, and you have already begun to share from your place of abundance by sharing your story. You are an exemplary person with a miraculous future ahead of you. I am excited for you in this.

I am sorry that you are hurting. I am acutely aware of how it feels to be arbitrarily chosen for marginalization. All I can do is offer my love and support, as well as to underscore my firm understanding that you will rise from these ashes and soar higher than you can know in this moment. Congratulations to you on your courage to speak publicly of your pain. Don't ever let anyone silence you.

Love and happiness,
Katie

Subject: Olivia's Letters

Dear Olivia,

I read about your story in the newspaper today. I'm so sorry to hear of the hard time you've been having in school. Some kids can be so hurtful sometimes. I wanted to tell you some advice I heard when I was in middle school and was being picked on. Bullies and kids who say mean things don't know the real you; if they did, they would not make fun of you. Bullies are people who are ignorant about themselves and others, and a lot of times they are insecure as well. Olivia, I'm sure you are a wonderful person, and for everyone who doesn't see that, well, you don't need 'em!! Don't live your life trying to impress others; live your life by impressing yourself.

Sincerely,
Camille

Dear Olivia,

I would like to begin by saying how sorry I am that you have had to go through these traumatic years. I can only imagine how you feel, because I myself have never truly been the victim of bullying, but I have much sympathy for you. I'm writing you mainly to tell you a little bit about my story. Throughout my middle school years, I became associated with what I could call the "wrong crowd." The girls I knew were vicious and would talk behind other people's backs, and the boys I knew/dated would not treat me with respect or gratitude. I was upset with the world and the way my classmates acted, and I was angry with myself because I could see that I was becoming just the kind of person I promised never to be.

My whole outlook on life changed the summer going into eighth grade when I met a friend who showed me that there really are goodhearted people out there, willing to help you and be there for you always. I'm telling you this all because I know that sometimes you must feel like giving up and just throwing in the towel. I know that you must feel like it's not worth it to go on with your everyday life because it can be not so good or even horrible, but I just want you to understand that someday you will find someone to change your perspective on life, someone to show you that even one great day can cancel out all the bad days you have experienced.

I hope that from now on your life is filled with happiness and you are able to live out every day with that beautiful smile I saw in the newspaper.

Kind regards and best wishes,

Helen

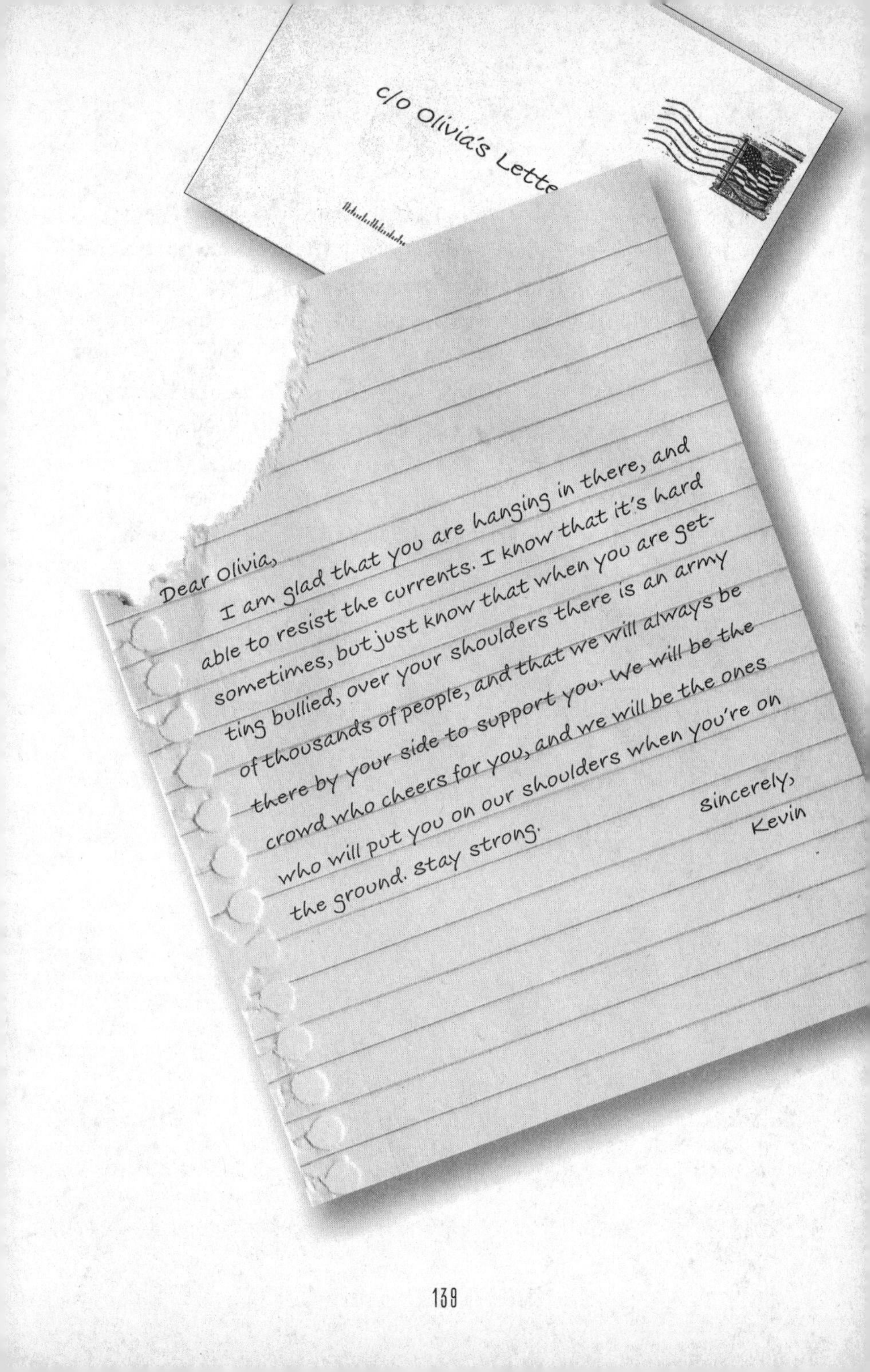
c/o Olivia's Lette

Dear Olivia,
I am glad that you are hanging in there, and able to resist the currents. I know that it's hard sometimes, but just know that when you are getting bullied, over your shoulders there is an army of thousands of people, and that we will always be there by your side to support you. We will be the crowd who cheers for you, and we will be the ones who will put you on our shoulders when you're on the ground. Stay strong.
Sincerely,
Kevin

Dear Olivia,

My name is Jasmine, and I am 14 years old, too. There are millions of girls and boys around the world who are bullied. To every single one of them, you are a hero. You've inspired tons of them to stand up and tell the bullies to step aside.

Nobody should ever be bullied! I think you've started a movement. You should start an organization, Olivia! I'd be more than happy to help. The sisters who started letter-writing campaign practically already started one for you. Olivia, I thank you for all that you are and for what you've done. Good luck, Olivia!

Yours truly,
Jasmine

Hi Olivia,

My uncle was epileptic, and I just felt that I needed to write to you. People are often afraid of difference or changes. The kids who were picking on you are ignorant, ignorant to the fact that it hurts to be made fun of. They wouldn't like it if they were the ones being made fun of. Remember that these are just kids and you will grow up and they will hopefully mature. We as humans go through things in our lives that will be handled one of two ways: they will make you bitter or they will make you better. If they make you bitter, you will take it out on everyone else or blame other people for what has happened. If they make you better, your personality will be one that people will want to be around. You'll be a person with a lot of hope in yourself and others. If you have any questions, just let me know.

God bless,
Michael

Subject: Olivia's Letters

Dear Olivia,

Going through your teenage years is one of the hardest things you'll ever face, and I think that most adults forget just how horrible it was for them. But one thing is certain, if you have people/pets around you that love you, and that you love back, you'll get through it. You'll find that when you get older, out of high school, out of college, the people who tormented you don't mean nearly as much anymore. They simply don't matter, because they're not worth it. Let them deal with their own lives, and make sure you make the most of yours.

The older you get, when the people you meet are more secure with who they are, the easier it is to find friends who are *real* friends, who will stick by you to the bitter end, who listen to you whine and cry, and who will make you laugh. Make sure that you're the best kind of person you can be, and the friends you make will be the kind of people you want to hang with.

Make sure to laugh every day, it's very relaxing, and good for you. Sing out loud, and dance around the room to your favorite music. Walk outside with friends or your dog. Spend time with your family. Find out what you're really good at, and do it. Find out what you want to do, and learn how. Spend time doing nothing. Do something nice for someone, just because.

It's easy to think that everyone is mean, but the letters that you're getting remind you (and us) that there are people out there who care, even if they don't know you.

Peace, sweetie,

Tracy

Dear Olivia:

I don't understand how other young adults can be so cruel—it doesn't make any sense to me but I know it happens.

As you stated, there are a hundred "kind" people for every unkind person in this world. I would like to add myself to your list of "kind" people.

Embrace your very individual "kindatude" and you will always be happy. You may ask, what is kindatude? Here is the definition:

kind-a-tude (noun): the state in which kindness and gratitude embrace each other to empower you to enrich your life and the lives of others, causing a ripple effect to make this world an extraordinary place. When you have a kind-a-tude you become the droplet that creates the ripple effect of kindness.

You are a very special young woman and a very strong young woman to have gone through what you have. I understand you are taking your struggles and heartaches and reaching out to others. That, Olivia, is a wonderful gesture and one you should be very proud of.

I wish the best for you in the future and for your mother as well.

Take care always and "become the droplet"!

Kathleen

Hi Olivia,

I read about you in the local newspaper and online, and I cried. Lots. Please believe me that I don't think of you as a victim. I think of you as a shining example of what can be done. Many, many people including myself have been bullied, and to be blunt, if I'd had your friends and the courage and determination YOU show, things would have been different.

Those that treated you badly just needed something to fill their otherwise empty lives. On the other hand, YOU are a shining star of hope for everyone else. Not just those who are being bullied, but for everyone, regardless of their age and background.

You are a remarkable young woman, and I sincerely hope that one day I'll be cheering at the end of your performance in theatre or dance, or whatever you choose to do.

I won't be applauding because you are a target of bullying, or just because you would have given a fabulous performance, but because you are setting a standard of hope, courage and determination for others to follow. And that is something that deserves more than praise; it deserves and gets respect and admiration.

All my hopes and dreams go with you,

Ian

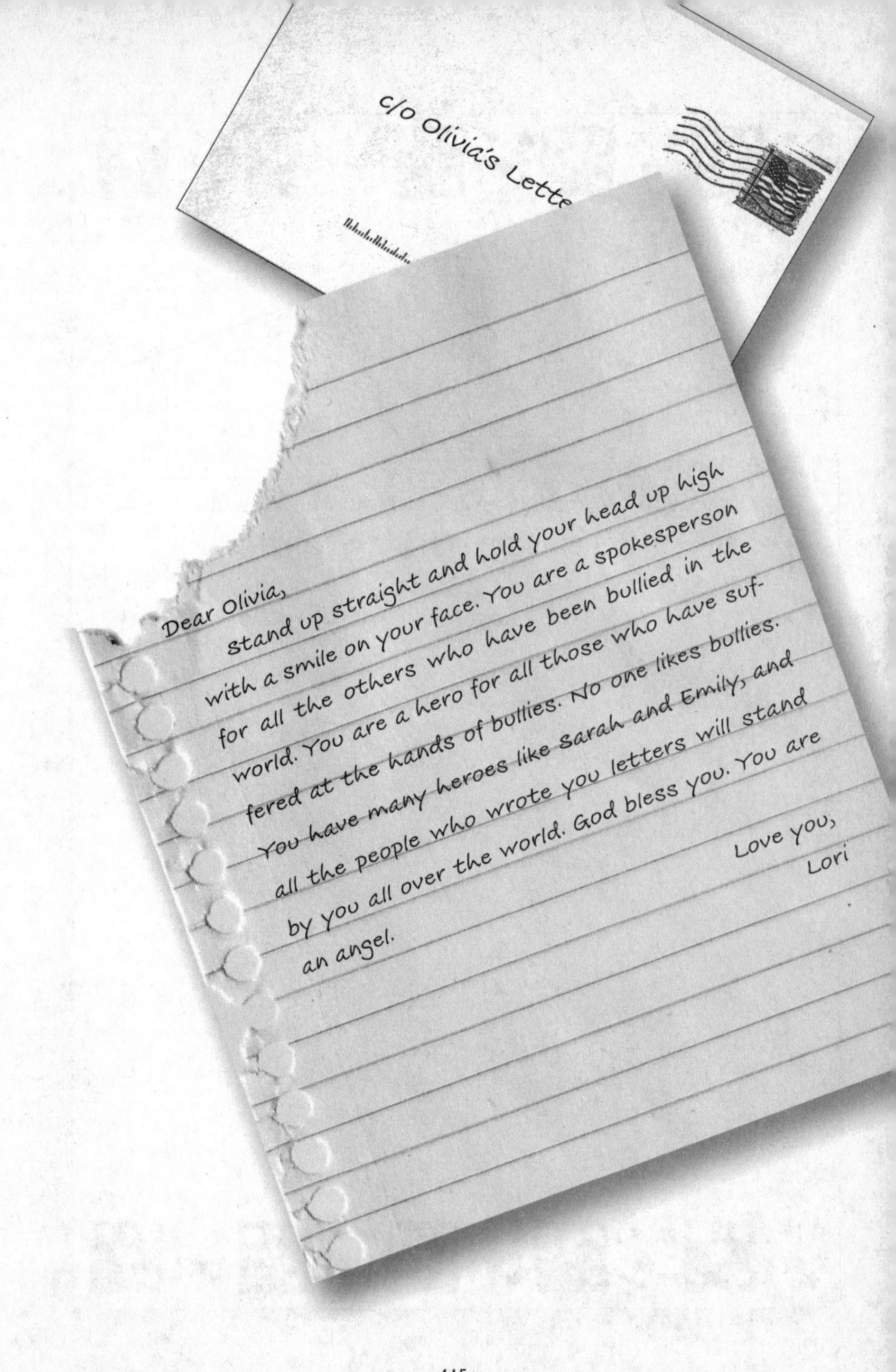

Dear Olivia,

Stand up straight and hold your head up high with a smile on your face. You are a spokesperson for all the others who have been bullied in the world. You are a hero for all those who have suffered at the hands of bullies. No one likes bullies. You have many heroes like Sarah and Emily, and all the people who wrote you letters will stand by you all over the world. God bless you. You are an angel.

Love you,
Lori

Dear Olivia,

I hope you are having a nice summer! I think about you a lot and I wish you all the best in the future.

God bless you!

Love, your friend you haven't met,
Leslie

Gosh, Olivia,

I'm so sorry to hear that you've felt so sad. Everyone feels sad and it really does feel awful sometimes. People can be really mean. But for every mean person there is a nice, kind person like yourself out there. I hope you find all those people. Tonight I'm going to say a little prayer that tomorrow is a better day for you.

Jennifer

Dear Olivia,

My name is Joan. I was overwhelmed with emotion reading your story and about the two sisters who decided to take action on your behalf.

Olivia, it does not matter that you do not know any of the people who are writing to you in the physical sense because spiritually we are all connected. This is why your story is affecting many from all over the world and we are writing you and sending you our love.

You have strength, compassion for others, love, and survival skills that many adults do not attain. These skills will serve you well in your life and I expect that the many wonderful things you do in your adulthood will be in part because of what you have experienced in your childhood.

Bullies are living in a world of fear, lack, and boredom, Olivia. This fear and lack result from feelings of being unloved, so to compensate bullies project these feelings onto anyone who they feel is fair game. Remove yourself from this pit of negative energy and let the love flow in. Replace any negative thoughts with positive and loving thoughts. Know yourself as being absolutely perfect and loving in every way.

I believe that your story will be published. Imagine, Olivia, at your young age how much you have already impacted the world. You are a miracle.

Love,
Joan

Subject: Olivia's Letters

Dear Olivia,

I have nothing magical to top what has already been started. The letters are such a simple and great idea to remind you that there are many more decent people out there than there are negative people.

However, I do have the pleasure of wishing you good luck in celebrating all your newfound support. Maybe someday you will be able to share some of the things you have learned from this experience and help another person get through a tough time.

May the force be with you, Olivia, Emily, and Sarah.

Bryan

c/o Olivia's Lette

To a brave young lady,

Congratulations, you have risen above those people. They are the ones with the problem, not you. Keep your chin up and show us what you're made of! Best of luck in your new future.

Julie

Dear Olivia,

I think you are a very strong girl. You did something I would never have done. You are the bravest person I know. You are not alone, Olivia! I can really learn from you. I would love to see all the great things you do one day.

Go Olivia!

Dear Olivia,

I read about you in the newspaper this morning and would like you to know that you are a hero of mine. I know you do not know me and that my requesting something of you is accordingly quite forward on my part, but I would like you to promise me that you will hold your head up high and realize that all difficult things do pass. And believe me, life is brimming with adversity—some good and some bad. A few years ago, I was diagnosed with cancer. After four operations and two bouts of radiation therapy, I beat the disease, and I now race bicycles like Lance Armstrong, finishing with the top riders in each of my races.

My difficult times dealing with what I had to deal with are but distant, fragmented memories that have waned with time and given me a new perspective on my life that has allowed me to focus on all the good that is in it—my family and friends who were at my bedside in the hospital, my health, each amazing day with its breadth of possibility. Those individuals who were unkind to you do not belong in your life. Think about it. If they were so easily persuaded by peer pressure to treat you so inappropriately when they knew it was wrong to do so, do you really want to devote your energies in cultivating friendships with them?

There are so many wonderful, trustworthy, considerate, and loving people in this world, and you will find the ones who will add to your life's richness. It may take some time, but be patient. You are a beautiful and courageous young lady whom many people look up to. You are helping them get through their own difficult times. So remember, promise me to hold your head up real high so everyone can see how good you are.

Your fan,
Salvatore

Subject: Olivia's Letters

Dear Olivia,

You are a beautiful person, and I am certain you will go on to do amazing things in this world. While the behavior of the other kids is a tragic example of our deteriorating society, do whatever you can to rise above them. They are not worth thinking about. I want you to know and believe that there are lots of people out there who, instead of hating, choose to value love, faith, and friendship. I believe you are one of them. I believe you have a strong will and capacity to turn the pain you've experienced into something positive. I believe that it won't be long before you are making a difference in the lives of others, and that your message will be one of love.

Diane

Dear Olivia,

I think the early teen years are so very hard for many young adults. My heart goes out to you because of the mistreatment and the horrible threats you have had to endure.

You have been told this before, but I believe it to be true: You have the inner strength to weather the trials that come your way. That strength will make you a much more compassionate person. Most importantly, the core of your personality will be so strong, that for the rest of your life other people will sense and respect your personal balance.

My very best to you and all (both young and old) who are the targets of bullies and others who "hate."

May your health improve. May you find a way to manage your epilepsy. May there be lots of sunshine and continued love in your future.

My best,

Inge

Dear Olivia,

Hello, Sunshine! Your story has touched the lives of many. May it open the eyes of others. You are an angel and a blessing to many.

May your journey through life be full of joy and happiness. Don't let anyone or anything stand in your way. You are loved by your parents, friends, and strangers, more than you'll ever know.

No matter where life takes you, honey, always love yourself and don't let nonsense bring you down.

Smile always,

Shannan

Subject: Olivia's Letters

Olivia,

I am a 55-year-old father of two. I have the greatest compassion for you and for others who have to face the sort of negative behavior that you did. I remember as a child growing up how I was bullied. I was "different" and people seem to fear difference. I remember my own daughter's anguish when others made fun of her awkwardness or physical differences. My son, too, was put down for his wit and intelligence.

It is indeed a terrible and confusing world that we live in where our diversity is put down instead of cherished. Where destructive actions and words are applauded and reinforced rather than shunned. I don't know if there are any answers to the issues of fear and anger.

I share with you what I shared with my kids and what was shared with me. Be true to yourself. Reacting to the negativity in life with more negative behavior just perpetuates the problem. Turning away from bullies, letting them rant and rave without reaction, is vastly more deflating to their ego than fighting back.

Be of good cheer, Olivia. You are in the company of friends.

Best wishes and follow your conscience,

Blaine

Dear Olivia,

It is with such deep thoughts and emotions that I write to you, for we are sisters in this world, sharing this same life experience.

The sadness I feel upon reading your story of torture and pain.

The sympathy I feel having lived through such an experience.

The shame I feel at having turned into a bully myself.

The gratitude I feel at having made amends for this transgression.

The utter awe and amazement that we are blessed with the gift of courage, caring, drive, and unselfishness from the dear ones who started this program.

The hope and inspiration upon remembering what our world can become.

Please always remember that people do change and love does heal. Keep your heart open and know that you are never alone in this life.

Blessings,

Katy

c/o Olivia's Lette

Dear Olivia,

I am a former teacher (middle and high school) and am SO sorry you were thrust into the middle of such a painful, totally unacceptable situation. I read a few articles about your struggle to find peace. I speak for probably thousands (or millions) of people who are outraged at the behavior of the bullies. Their hearts must be hard, but I hope if enough people speak out against such toxic behavior, goodness still has a chance to win in the world. You are a brave, beautiful, sensitive girl, and I know your pain can transcend to help heal the world. God bless!

Patricia

Dear Olivia,

What a wonderfully inspiring story about the compassion two sisters had for you and the change it made in your life!

The good news for you is that you have learned far more about yourself and your worth and your strength than the bullies who found such pleasure from their behavior. You are growing into an incredibly aware person who believes in herself and her values. You have made a difference in the lives of thousands of young people who may have endured bullying, too.

May God bless and keep you and your beautiful mom in good health—both mental and physical. And may you always know that you have made an amazing difference in this world.

Best,
Trish

Dear Olivia,

I just read your story, and I wanted to tell you to be strong and lean on those around you who love you. One day you will look back on this and it will just be a bad memory as you move on to do bigger and better things. Those people who bully and put others down are so small, and if they continue being the way they are, they will always remain small. You persevered despite them.

Keep it up!

Andrea

Dear Olivia,

My name is Brooke, and I read an article about you in the newspaper. Your story made me feel sad and realize how bad bullying can be. I want you to know that it doesn't matter what bullies think, just as long as you feel good about yourself and you know you're a good person.

Love,

Brooke

Dear Olivia,

My name is Justin. I am 13 years old. I have heard about your hard situation, but I have one tip for you. This is that humor heals all wounds.

Sincerely,
Justin

Dear Olivia,

I cannot say I am surprised at your story. All my life I have witnessed incredible cruelty propagated by teens and preteens toward their peers who are "not cool."

What is odd, almost unbelievable, is that the same kids who are so horrible in middle school and high school grow up to be normal adults—even good ones—kind, generous, concerned. And, in fact, if you ask every adult you know how they were treated in middle school and high school, I guarantee at least half will say they were unpopular or an outcast. I do know the scars last a long time. I have no advice for you, no easy answers.

But just remember that it is not your fault and that there are people who care about you, who are touched by your story, people you don't even know. I'm sure that other kids and parents who read your story will see themselves or their kids in you. And maybe one or two of your tormentors will see themselves, and be ashamed of what they did.

Take care, Olivia and mom, and be well.

Dan

Dear Olivia,

I'm a high school English teacher in San Francisco. My eleventh grade class just finished reading the newspaper story on your situation, and we all feel compelled to respond to you directly. Your bravery is inspiring.

We marvel at anyone strong enough to experience what you have been through. Young teenagers (middle-schoolers) have a tendency to be incredibly cruel. As teenagers, we want you to know it gets better. For most teenagers, by the time they reach high school, a lot of that insecurity has diminished. In fact, we would be honored to have you here at our school when the time comes for you to start high school.

Thank you for your inspiration!

Mr. Jordan's class

Subject: Olivia's Letters

Dear Olivia,

I just had to tell you how much I admire you. What a strong person you must be! You have been through things that would bring many adults to their knees. I work in a local emergency room as a nurse, and I am constantly saddened by the number of kids brought in who have tried to kill themselves. Almost without exception, the child has been bullied. It is sad that so many seem to need to put others down in order to feel good about themselves. My own daughter (who is 13) went through a time when she was bullied by a couple of boys at her school, and my heart ached to see her going through that. I went through some of the same type of treatment when I was in school, too.

I can still remember how much it hurt. I am so glad that those two sisters reached out to you. And you are right. There *are* a hundred good people out there for every bad person. You are a beautiful girl, obviously intelligent and mature beyond your years, and you have a heart of gold that just shines through. Instead of letting the bullies ruin your life, you have taken those horrible experiences and turned them into something positive. You have shown a strength of character and resolve that many can only hope to aspire to. You are undoubtedly an inspiration to all those kids out there who have been through bullying.

By sharing your experience, you are raising awareness of the problem of bullying and hopefully showing some apparently ignorant parents out there that such behavior isn't just "normal for middle school." Your mother must be very proud of you, and her love for you must be a great source of comfort and strength. You are obviously an extraordinary young lady. I know you will go far in life with all of the wonderful qualities you possess. Best of luck to you and your mother; may God bless you both for sharing this terrible experience and touching the hearts of so many people.

Big hugs you to, your mom, and to those two sisters who reached out to you.

Love,

Becky

Hi Olivia,

I'm a police officer in North Carolina. For a year I worked in the schools as a school resource officer and I came to realize how hard it is for children who get picked on. There's a fine line between jokes, teasing, and horseplay and pure mean-spirited bullying. Certainly getting picked on for a medical condition and having your personal belongings dragged through the mud is beyond the scope of any joke.

Fortunately, it's not like that in every situation. We had a young man named Bart in our school who was actually mentally handicapped. Happily for Bart, everyone did their best to support him and encourage him. There were some incidents of silliness, but none of it was spiteful, and Bart seemed to enjoy the attention. I sometimes had a dim view of kids because I was always dealing with the bad ones, but the way the students looked after Bart was very encouraging.

All the best,
John

Dear Olivia,

I was bullied when I was a kid, and hearing your story brought tears to my eyes thinking about what you went through. I am so sorry this happened to you.

I was glad to hear that those two young ladies started writing to you, and that you have received so much support.

There are two things I want you to know. One is that the vast majority of people are good, and the second thing is that you did nothing wrong that brought on this behavior. You are not to blame for their behavior. They are.

All the best to you,

Don

Dear Olivia,

You know the saying "sticks and stones may break my bones, but names will never hurt me." If only this were true! In fact, being judged harshly, being teased unmercifully, being made fun of for how we look or for who we are or even for how others perceive us, often inflicts deep and lasting wounds.

The good news is that bullying is finally receiving the attention it warrants. We are recognizing that bullying creates more bullying, is one of the main triggers of depression, suicide, and drug abuse for teens, and often creates a lifetime of disorders that hinder people from living the extraordinary lives they deserve.

Bullying is a cycle we can stop in so many ways as the Buder family, you, and others are showing us. First, just as we have done with sexual abuse and molestation, we must take it out of our collective closet, shine the light on it, call it by its name, and let those who have experienced it know that they need not carry any shame. We must not turn the other cheek, ignore it, or tell those who are bullied that someday it will get better. This only teaches sufferers to endure loneliness, shame, humiliation, rage, and self-hate. Loneliness can become a habit. Shame can become a habit. By naming bullying we take away the power of the secret. We become islands in the stream for those who have suffered from bullying, safe havens where they can rest, release, relax, and rebuild.

Second, we must open our eyes. We must commit to noticing not just the bullying behaviors but the symptoms of those who are being bullied. Anyone who is depressed, self-destructive, accident-prone, suicidal, anxiety-ridden, doing poorly at work or in school, has difficulty concentrating, has low self-esteem, or has addictions, may be suffering from bullying now or in the past. If you have the courage to ask them if they have been or are being bullied, you may find that they have the courage and the desire to share their secret with you. When I have reason to be suspicious that a new client has been sexually abused, I have often just asked straight out. I can't tell you how many times I have heard this response, "Oh, my God. How did you know? I've never told anyone, not even my (therapist/husband/minister)." Few want to live with this secret. Most think they have no other choice.

Third, we must stop seeing the situation in simplistic terms, categorizing people into perpetrators and victims. We must realize that anyone who bullies may have been bullied themselves. If we simply criminalize bullies, particularly teenagers who exhibit these disturbing behaviors, we will be missing thousands and thousands who need our help. The cycle of bullying will break when we reach out with compassion to everyone—bullies and bullied alike. This doesn't mean that we should tolerate bullying. On the contrary, we should have zero tolerance for words and deeds that are hurtful.

Jane

Subject: Olivia's Letters

Dear Olivia,

As a psychologist who has been in practice for over fifteen years, I have been privileged to be invited into the private emotional lives of many wonderful patients. These patients include children, adolescents, and adults who have come in search of some relief from the emotional pain and intrusive symptoms that may be impeding their lives. While some problems can be dealt with in the here and now, others involve traumatic experiences from the past. All too often adults in my practice, both men and women, have revealed that chronic bullying by peers constituted a major emotional trauma in their childhood. In fact, my practice is composed of many people who, as children, were relentlessly bullied and they are still talking about it!

My patients share stories of being bullied on the playground, on the school bus, on the walk home from school, and at summer camp. They describe experiences of being physically and/or emotionally bullied, both leaving them feeling frightened, helpless, and alone. Descriptions of being verbally tortured on a daily basis, of peers constantly peeking over the bathroom stall, and of threats of bodily harm are what I have heard. Though these experiences took place sometimes twenty, thirty, and in some cases, forty years ago, the emotional pain continues to resonate in their current lives. It is important to note that the effects of chronic bullying can be profound and long-lasting.

I have observed a variety of different ways in which people are impacted by their chronic bullying experiences. There are those who seem to have dealt with the bullying by becoming vigilant and are on alert much of the time. These people are reactive and perceive minor slights as major injuries. They may spend a good deal of their energies fighting the metaphorical bullies they see everywhere. There are others who seem more overtly insecure. Their self-confidence is compromised and their sense of trust in others is shaken. There is a perceived sense of doom and danger and this bleeds much of the joy out of engaging with the world at large. While the presentations may vary, the underlying issues tend to be similar. Most express a sense of self as damaged and a sense of the environment as unsafe.

Many of my patients seem to have internalized the negative messages perpetuated by the chronic bullies. They think that there is something innately wrong with them and that is why they have been singled out. They feel unattractive, unworthy, and cowardly. Even when the reality contradicts their negative internalized messages, they hold on to them. Even though the actual bully is out of the picture, the bully is now inside of them. Much of the work tends to center around ridding oneself of this internal bully, a bully who one now has more control over.

While there are many factors that bring one to therapy, the impact of stressors during one's youth cannot be underestimated. Many assume that being bullied is simply a normative childhood rite of passage. They may think that it is something that makes the child stronger. While it is appropriate to teach children good coping skills and to help them to learn to use their voice, situations involving chronic bullying require adult intervention. It is apparent to me that the lack of effective adult intervention in these chronic bullying situations is what ultimately exacerbates the experience and thus leaves the door wide open for trauma.

Chronic bullying needs to be taken seriously. Teaching children to know what constitutes bullying and to be proactive when they see it occurring can be helpful steps. Encouraging children to speak up whether they are the target or a witness to the bullying can create an environment of support and decrease the likelihood of apathy. Parents and relevant adults must be involved in the process of responding to a chronic bullying situation. In my patients' thoughts I can hear their concerns as to why no one stepped in to protect them. Did they not care? Was I not good enough? Is there no power strong enough to defeat this bully?

Kelly

Dear Olivia,

The Olivia's Letters campaign is a wonderfully creative response to the dreadful problem of bullying in our schools. This campaign could provide a positive model for other efforts to combat the epidemic of bullying in schools and over the Internet.

Bullies thrive when the community doesn't take an unequivocal stand against their behavior. By helping to provide such overwhelming positive support for you, the Buder family has powerfully shown that love can speak with a clearer and stronger voice than hatred.

This project is shining a spotlight on the epidemic of bullying in our schools, locally and nationally. It is my hope that administrators, teachers, and parents will unite to take an effective stand against this damaging practice.

I urge people to spread the word about the Olivia's Letters campaign so that similar support efforts can spring up to provide help to other students who have been targeted by bullying. This problem is definitely nationwide.

Sincerely,
Norman

Dear Olivia:

I read your story and wanted to let you know that I too was bullied. I won't go into details but suffice it to say the scars are still with me, and I am 38 years old now. It affected my self-esteem, my relationships—everything. You are not alone. Also know, although at this point it may be of little consolation, that some bullies are cowards who may not like themselves and take it out on others believing that will make them feel better about themselves. It doesn't.

You are a true hero in all of this, and don't you ever forget it. You have also been given a unique opportunity to help educate others, as well as yourself and help change behaviors and maybe someone's life for the better. You may even make the bullies stop and think and change the way they treat others and themselves. Take advantage of that opportunity, for many people never get the chance you have been given—to make a serious and positive change in the world.

I know it's hard, especially as a kid, to turn a negative into a positive, but you can do it. My thoughts and prayers are with you.

Best of luck,

Christopher

My dear Olivia,

By now the flood of mail has probably enabled you to see that you are a good person who just happened to become the victim of some very unpleasant characters. Perhaps soon you'll even truly realize how much better it is to be you than it would be to be one of them.

Are you familiar with the term "ripple effect," referring to the circle of ripples which forms around the spot where a pebble is tossed into a pond? Well, you seem to have become a one-woman ripple effect. Think of all the positive actions that have emerged from this initial bad treatment of you. Many, many people have stopped to consider bullying and the disastrous results it can have. More than four thousand people have taken the time to write and tell you that their hearts are with you. Some may even have related long-buried stories of their own sufferings at the hands of bullies. Others may take strength from your story and find the courage to stand up and defend someone who is being picked on unfairly. Maybe even one or more of those who tormented you for so long may now be suffering deserved guilt pangs and deciding to stop the bullying.

Who knows where these events will end?

Olivia, I wish you a long and happy life, secure in the sense of your own worth.

BJ

Dear Olivia,

I'm 37 years old now, but when I was in high school, I was bullied both verbally and physically. That was over twenty years ago. There have been several stories both online and in the news about the subject, and I find myself saying "It's about time." When I was a freshman, bullying was what I term a transparent issue, meaning it was pretty much the norm for schools and no one really did anything about it. I saw your story on the news and the outpouring of support you received, and I thought, having been there, I would like to show my support for you and anyone else being victimized by this in our schools.

Adults say "Ignore them, and they will go away." It isn't true. In my personal experience, ignoring them only makes it worse. The problem has got to be dealt with.

Joseph

Dear Olivia,

I'm just writing to let you know that you stand for courage and hope for many girls who are the targets of evil bullying. Thank you for your bravery. You will change the world! I don't know you, but I am very proud of you and think you rock!!!

Best,
Jennifer

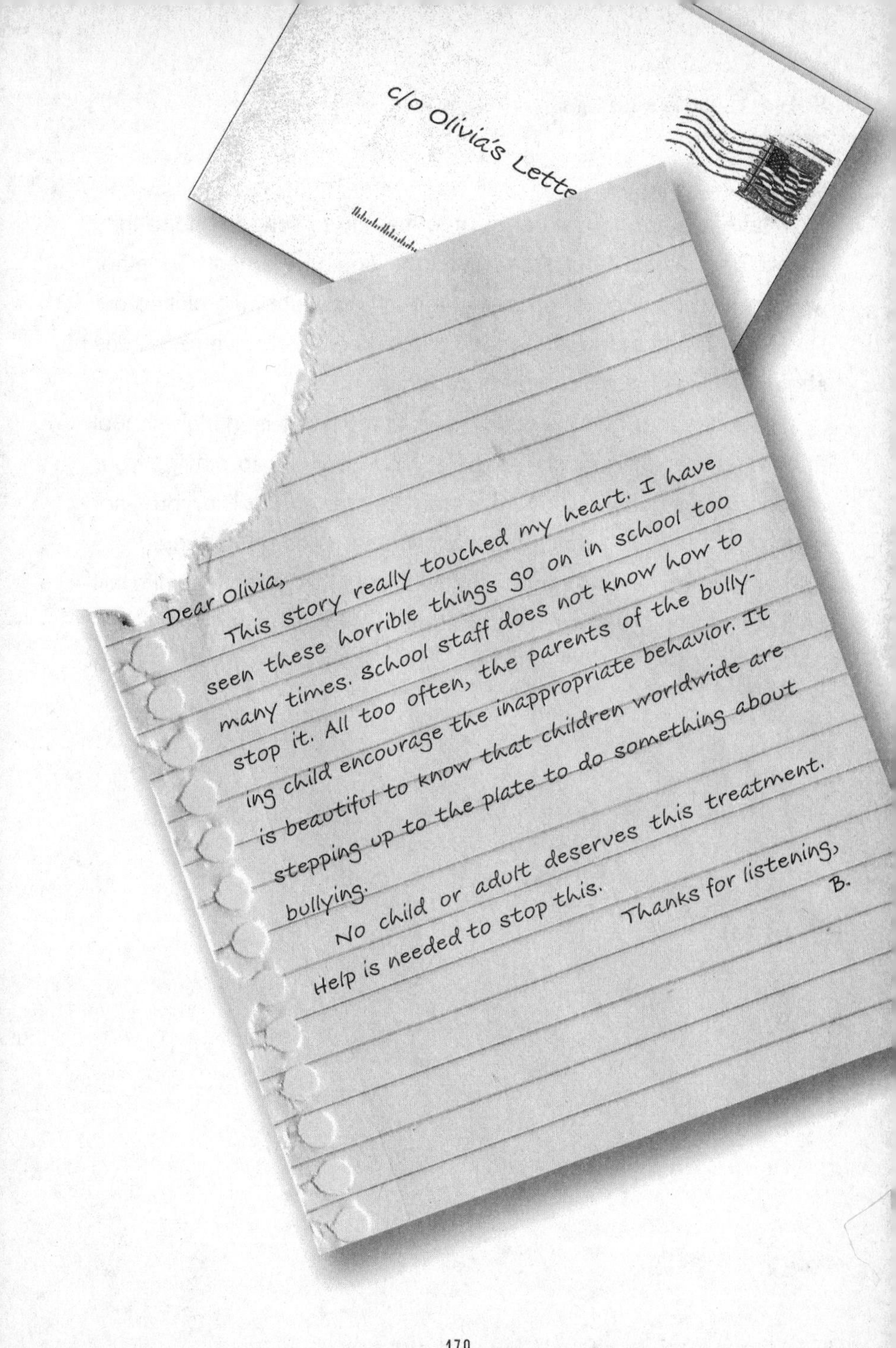

Dear Olivia,

This story really touched my heart. I have seen these horrible things go on in school too many times. School staff does not know how to stop it. All too often, the parents of the bullying child encourage the inappropriate behavior. It is beautiful to know that children worldwide are stepping up to the plate to do something about bullying.

No child or adult deserves this treatment. Help is needed to stop this.

Thanks for listening,

B.

Subject: Olivia's Letters

Dear Olivia,

I have two young children. When they go to school, I hope they do not get bullied. Your story gives me encouragement. Together we can hold each other up and stand tall against being picked on, singled out, and made to feel bad. Now I feel like I have resources should my kids have a similar experience.

My son is four and plays drums, and my niece is in high school and writes her own music on guitar and cello. Keep playing your keyboard and guitar. Many, many artists started life like you—not exactly "popular" in school, but they went on to do great things!

I am one of many who hope that with time this part of your life will be just a memory and your life will be full of happiness.

Beth

Dear Olivia,

I just saw your story on the "Today" show, and I wanted to write and tell you how proud I am that you are helping others through your adversity. You are an inspiration and a miracle. I have always been disgusted by any person who would bully another; it's cruel and truly evil. How refreshing to see you and a band of other young people finally say "NO!" and take a stand against this vile act. You are an extremely special young woman and I know you are going to grow into a nurturing, caring adult with integrity. You are making a difference in this world!

Thank you, and bless you.

Kim

Hi Olivia,

You are my hero. I am amazed at how well you've handled the bullying. You are so mature at such a young age.

I'm sorry to hear about all the pain you've endured at the hands of your classmates. Kids can be cruel at times, but most are pretty nice.

Many, many years ago I also had similar problems at my school but my circumstances just helped to change my perspective on life.

Look at all the people you've helped. Not many kids, never mind adults, have such a positive impact on so many others. Because of your efforts, countless other kids won't have to endure what you had to.

That's why you're my hero.

God bless,
Gary

c/o Olivia's Lette

Dear Olivia,

I am writing because, perhaps, if more people speak out against bullying, and know that it's going on, it may become a little more difficult for bullies to bully.

Good luck to you, Olivia. I know it takes a very long time to get over bullying. It is very hard. Good luck!

Diana

Olivia,

Hey!!! Well, my name is Raquel, and today my teacher told us about your story. I was really amazed and really, really, really encouraged. I thought that you were so brave and that what you've done is really going to help a lot of people who have gone through and are going through what you have. I have never been bullied before, but now whenever I see someone getting bullied, I'm going to be sure that I stick up for that person. Yup, yup. And I'm sure you've heard this before, but you really shouldn't listen to negative things people have to say because it's so not worth it. And I know that you don't know me at all and it's kind of weird to say this, but if you ever need anything or you just need to talk, I'm here, OK?

With respect,

Raquel

Subject: Olivia's Letters

Dear Olivia,

Hello and what a powerful story! Many positive thoughts and supportive prayers headed your way for what you have been through and for how you've made a bad situation into a more positive one.

I just wanted to let you know that there are some public middle schools that really are making an effort to keep bullying out of school. I've had the good fortune to work at a middle school that takes a proactive stance on bullying and harassment of any kind. We have a great counselor who has an annual presentation for the students about bullying, harassment, and taunting. We also educate teachers on how to identify bullying going on in their classes and around the school, who to report it to, and what else can be done about it.

The difference between a school that sees bullying as "normal" and one that doesn't tolerate it is education. Many people see bullying as "just a phase" teenagers go through; few people stop and think that while it's true that it's a "phase," that still does *not* make it acceptable! Parents, students, school administrators, and teachers should all understand that it is unacceptable behavior.

It isn't surprising that teens bully each other, but that still doesn't make it right to excuse it as "just a phase." It's like saying everyone who gets a new car is going to go through a "road rage phase" and we all just have to tolerate it. It's like saying someone who just turned 21 is going to go through a "drunk-driving stage" and we all just have to put up with it! Please know that there are teachers like me who go out of our way to tell middle schoolers that bullying is “low-class, rude, and shows you have no manners” (yes, those are the actual words I use. :)

I know your Olivia’s Letters project can and will make a difference in the lives of many children and make their journey through the early teens an easier one. :)

Laura

Dear Olivia,

I saw the article about your story and wanted to be a part of this project, even though I am on the other end of the age spectrum from you, as I have grandchildren your age. My purpose in writing is to support you in treasuring the love you give and receive each day from trusted friends and family.

I am truly sorry that you have had the difficult experience of being the target of kids who have bullied and disrespected you. Learning that some people build themselves up by tearing down others is painful. It is hard to say exactly why this happens, but it is unacceptable.

My professional work is in human resources, which means that, among other things, I enforce the laws that protect people from bullying and harassment at work. I inform people that they cannot act or talk in disrespectful ways to other employees or they will lose their job. And you know what: I love it!! I enjoy having the role of the enforcer of safety for all. I am quick to say: "You can act anyway you like at home, but when you are at work, you will drop your prejudice, silly games, and make this a safe place for everyone!"

The day will come when the whole world will be a safe place for all people; I hope I live to see it.

Best to you,

Laura

c/o Olivia's Lette

Dear Emily and Sarah,

Bravo to you sisters for standing up for Olivia against the bullies. She needs all the help and encouragement she can get. You are doing a wonderful service to let people know that bullying is very antisocial behavior and needs to be stopped everywhere it pops up its ugly head.

My message to Olivia is this: People all over the world care about you and know you will be strong enough to hold your head high and ignore those ignorant bullies.

Keep up the good work.

Lorraine

Hi Olivia,

I saw you on TV today and, believe me, at first look I think you're such a beautiful lady. I know how difficult it must be to have an illness like yours, it's so hard to function in a normal way, but there are a lot of people like you, who in spite of a condition still found success. Illness in whatever form should not hinder us from fulfilling our dreams and becoming who we want to be.

Life is great and beautiful so we should make the most of it. You're still young, enjoy life, never let yourself be bothered by other people who just want to make things complicated for you. So cheer up, smile, God loves you. Just pray and I hope you'll have a good future ahead of you.

God bless. Hope this e-mail gets to you.

Regards from a friend,
Marj

Dear Olivia,

Hi there, it seems strange that a story on the news would prompt me to write a letter. I have lived my whole childhood thinking I was a second-class person. For whatever reason, others singled me out. I spent all that time thinking it was my fault and that, maybe, if I only tried a little harder, I could fit in. I realize now that nothing I could have done would have stopped the bullies. But back then I was a very bitter person and I spent a good part of my life mad at everyone I came into contact with. The birth of my daughter four years ago made me realize that I have wasted my time being hurt. I allowed myself to screw up my life trying to get all the anger and frustration out. Please don't let those few weak people bring you down. As you have seen already, there are millions of us out there in the same place you are now and, believe me, it does get better and I am glad to know that you have the support of all these people. I never got that and I let the hate take me over. Please don't let them change who you are.

The world is with you.

Heidi

Subject: Olivia's Letters

Dear Olivia,

I can only imagine the pain you have been feeling these past few years. I am deeply saddened by how you were taunted because you had a seizure. I am so very sorry. I will be praying for you and sending positive healing thoughts your way. I have boy/girl twins who are 10 years old and I shudder to think of them or their friends being bullied the way you have been. I teach my kids to be kind to everyone and to include others. In my work as a psychologist, I help teens who have been bullied and I have been leading parent education groups at my children's school. I am speaking out against bullying in my work and there are many other psychologists who are doing the same.

Please know you are not alone and that your own speaking out is helping you heal and getting others involved. Together, we can end bullying and social exclusion. Take good care of yourself and never stop pursuing your dreams.

Sincerely,

Robin

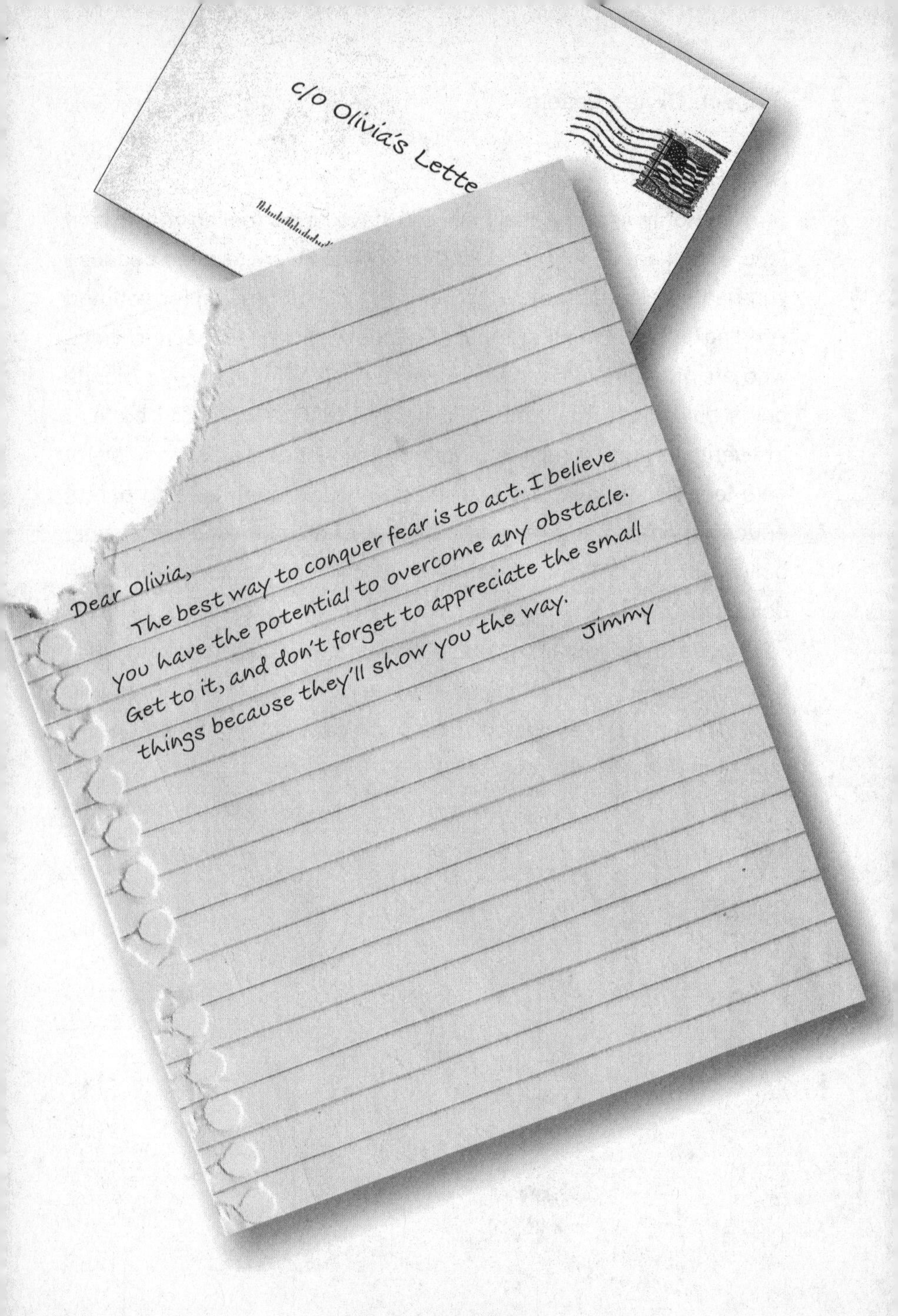

LETTERS TO A BULLIED GIRL

Dear Olivia,

I heard your story the other day from my mom. So I looked up more information and figured out how I could personally write to you. I found a website that said people were writing you notes of empathy. That's not what I want to write to you. I want to thank you. Thank you for inspiring and encouraging people like myself. Thank you for not taking your own life and letting those who hurt you win. Thank you for being strong and beautiful inside and out. I don't know you, but you are willing to tell your story and I can't imagine how many kids, teenagers, and adults who are abused and harassed who feel alone. It's nice to see the world coming together and it's all because of you. You being brave enough to share your story. That is more strength and bravery than sometimes I think I could ever have. So thank you. Even though I've said it a hundred times now, thank you. I think you'll grow up and have a great life, and just imagine the stories you'll be able to tell! I know if I was getting thousands of letters a day, they would start to run together. But I hope you are able to see this letter and remember that you helped one person.

Thank you so much,

Lisa

Dear Olivia,

My name is Jessica. I am in elementary school. My teacher read us the newspaper article about you being bullied. It made me sad when I heard how kids were treating you. If I was the principal, they would not be in school. Say to your bullies that that have no right to do that to you. I think it's great how you talked to people instead of keeping it inside. You are a nice girl, and I know that from the heart. I wish I could meet you and be friends with you. We could play dolls and have tea parties.

Your friend who you haven't met yet,

Jessica

Dear Olivia,

I cannot say I am surprised at your story. All my life I have witnessed incredible cruelty propagated by teens and preteens toward their peers who are "not cool." What is odd, almost unbelievable, is that the same kids who are so horrible in middle school and high school grow up to be normal adults—even good ones—kind, generous, concerned. And, in fact, if you ask every adult you know how they were treated in middle school and high school, I guarantee at least half will say they were unpopular, or an outcast. I do know the scars last a long time—maybe forever.

I have no advice for you, no easy answers. Just remember Olivia: "It's not your fault."

Stupidity, cruelty, and evil have been with us since the dawn of time. Look at all the wars, the hatred, the killings, the brutality. Then look at a tree, a sunset, a flower—it is still a beautiful world.

Remember also that there are people who care about you, who are touched by your story, people you don't even know. I'm sure that other kids and parents who read your story will see themselves or their kids. And maybe one or two of your tormentors will see themselves and be ashamed of what they did.

Take care,

Dan

APPENDIX

How to Start Your Own Letter-writing Campaign

Many people have contacted us requesting information about how to launch a letter-writing campaign like "Olivia's Letters." We have already worked with several families who have initiated successful projects in their own communities. There are many benefits that result from this kind of community effort. Most importantly, encouraging and compassionate messages seem to reduce the overriding sense of loneliness that bullied children often feel. Receiving supportive feedback from their peers helps to improve their self-esteem and raise their spirits. The letters also provide an opportunity for others to take a stand against bullying.

We recommend the following list of steps to initiate an anti-bullying letter-writing campaign in your community.

- If you are planning to write letters for someone else's child, contact the parent(s) and get permission to proceed.

- Decide which school(s) within the community you will ask to contribute letters.

- Develop a letter or e-mail to send to the school community (including school administrative staff and teachers) informing them of the purpose of the project and providing specific instructions on how to write and send letters (see our sample letter below).

- Contact the principal(s) of the school(s) to obtain permission to launch the project. Also obtain permission from the principal to have the head of the PTA (or whoever is responsible for sending out bulk mailings) send your e-mail to the entire school community. If e-mail is not an available form of communication, you will need to send a bulk mailing to all the home addresses of the families.

- Set up a P.O. box in your town to receive any letters that are mailed. Also ask the parent(s) of the bullied child to set up their own P.O. box so they have a confidential mailing address to receive the letters you forward.

- Decorate a box with the project title on it and put it in a conspicuous place in the main office of the school (don't forget to alert the school secretary!).

- E-mail your letter to the PTA head who can then send it off to the entire school community. We asked everyone to begin letters with "Dear Olivia" and sign letters using only a first name and age to protect confidentiality. It is best to offer people different ways to send the letters (e-mail directly to you, mail letters to your P.O. Box, drop letters off in a designated box in the main office of the school).

- Check the school box and your P.O. box daily to collect letters.

- Prepare a number of packages in advance and decorate them with stickers and colorful markers so that the package you send filled with letters is bright and inviting.

- Screen the letters for appropriate content before forwarding them to the child's P.O. box. Send no more than ten to fifteen letters a day so that the child will not be overwhelmed and can better appreciate the quality of each letter.

- If you would like to expand your project, contact principals of other schools in your county to get their students involved as well.

The E-mail That Launched "Olivia's Letters"

To all parents and students:

Many of you may have read about the recent experience of a girl named Olivia Gardner, who encountered very mean-spirited and relentless bullying in school as well as on the Internet. Olivia's mother changed her school three times yet the bullying, particularly on the Internet, grew more widespread. Olivia is now having to be homeschooled and is emotionally distraught.

In response to this concerning incident and the growing wave of bullying occurring through the anonymous medium of cyberspace, we are launching a project called "Olivia's Letters" which we hope you will be a part of. We are asking all parents to discuss this incident with their kids and ask them to write a letter to Olivia consisting of positive, encouraging, and reassuring words that would help boost her spirits, improve her self-worth, and restore faith in her peers.

Our goal is to collect hundreds of letters and begin to send them in doses next week to a P.O. box that Olivia's mother has set up for this purpose. Olivia's mother is incredibly touched by our school's efforts to help her daughter and hopes that these supportive letters from her peers will help Olivia get through this difficult time. We are also hoping to extend the scope of this project. We greatly appreciate your participation in this endeavor and hope to receive your student's letter as soon as possible. Thank you so much.

Sincerely,

Emily Buder and Sarah Buder

We Receive Permission from Olivia's Mother

Dear Janet, Emily and Sarah's mom,

I am Olivia's mother and I cannot tell you how touched I am by your idea. Olivia is in sooo much pain right now. She has been taken out of school by her therapist and physician and she is feeling very isolated; especially since she is an only child. The project you proposed where your girls collect letters of encouragement is one of the best things that I think could happen to Olivia right now. To hear from her peers is much more powerful than what "mom" says. The hateful energy is still being directed at her and she is really doubting herself. You have my permission to let the girls be our angels on earth and do this kind endeavor. Thank you for being who you are.

Kathleen, Olivia's mom

Our First Letters to Olivia

Dear Olivia,

I've started and erased this letter so many times; I don't even know how to start saying what I want to say to you. I really hope that you are taking all of these letters to heart, and knowing that there are a great deal of people in this world who dearly care about you, even if we don't know you personally. Each and every one of our hearts reach out to you and feel for you, for you have undergone much more pain in the few years of your life than a lot of people do in an entire lifetime. I hope you will listen to this one thing I have to say to you, it would mean the world to me: you are a strong, unique, outstanding individual and I hope you say this to yourself every morning when you get out of bed. "I am myself, I love myself, and nobody else can change that."

I cannot even begin to comprehend how people can be so cruel; I don't see the point and I couldn't even imagine living the lifestyle of a bully. I'm sure a lot of people have told you it's because they are jealous or immature, and that could be true, but besides that, it comes down to one simple thing: they really have nothing better to do with their lives. I hope someday they will look back on themselves and see what a pathetic waste of time this was. The best thing you can do is not let it affect you. Think of it this way: people like that aren't even worth your thoughts. These bullies want power, and the best thing to do in this situation is not give it to them. Stay strong. The best way to fight back hate is with love.

My heart is with you.

Peace and love,
Sarah Buder, age 14

Dear Olivia,

Words cannot express how much I admire you. Middle school is a rough patch in life for everyone, but I can't imagine the kinds of terrible things you have experienced throughout this stage in your life. I hope you have not lost faith in the general goodness of people. There are so many good people in the world, but unfortunately it seems to be the bad ones who have the most impact on the course of our lives. Throughout middle school, everyone is trying to find his or her place. Sometimes people get so caught up in trying to fit in and prove themselves to their peers that morality becomes skewed and people begin to turn on others just because they simply have nowhere else to turn. You did not deserve anything that the bullies said or did to you. They became so wrapped up in their group mentality that they chose random targets to take their internal frustrations out on, and you just happened to be one of those targets. Nothing about you warrants this kind of cruelty. These people who have harmed you will hopefully realize one day the kind of hurt that they have caused you and whomever else they may have bullied.

As hard as it may be, try not to take this bullying to heart. Please don't ever doubt your value as a person just because of these bullies, because that is exactly what they want you to do. By doubting yourself, you are giving them the power over you that they want in order to feel better about themselves. If you stay strong and believe that you are a genuinely wonderful and amazing person (as I'm sure you are), then you have the power over the bullies and you have shown the world what a strong person you are. Just by keeping your head up throughout this entire situation, you have proven to everyone around you the kind of strong-willed and wholesome person that you are. You have demonstrated qualities that most adults don't even possess—perseverance, courage, and the will to move forward onto better things.

However much this experience has diminished your faith in the good of humankind, please try to remember that there are people who are on your side, who care about you immensely, and who admire you for the strength you have shown by pushing through this. You are a beautiful, wonderful, and strong person, and all of us who care about you will be here to help you get through this. Things will *get better—in high school kids become less judgmental and less group-oriented, and I'm sure you will find an amazing group of friends who will genuinely care about you and never let anything like this happen to you ever again. Please keep your head up and never doubt yourself. You have a bright future ahead of you!*

Emily Buder, age 17

ACKNOWLEDGMENTS

We would like to thank those at our publisher, HarperCollins, including Amy Kaplan and Lisa Sharkey, for conceiving the idea of this book and for facilitating its publication. We appreciate how interested and supportive you all were of its message. Very special thanks to Amy Kaplan, our editor, for your skill in organizing and editing the book's content. You are a gentle but firm taskmaster, and we are grateful for your patience. You are also a pleasure to work with!

To Amy Rennert, our literary agent, thank you for all your professional guidance and support in bringing this book project together. You were always ready and willing to answer our questions at a moment's notice. Also, thanks to Robyn Russell Blanchette for helping us obtain releases.

Thank you to Emily and Sarah's principal, Chris Holleran of Tamalpais High School in Mill Valley, California, as well as all the teachers at Tam High for your enthusiastic support of this project and for encouraging students to participate. A special thanks to Yvonne Milham for helping to promote the project within the school and Jayne Greenberg, PTA President, for sending our e-mail to the school community. We so appreciate Allison Hrivoruchko, school receptionist, who guarded our "Dear Olivia" box in the main office and encouraged students to contribute letters daily.

To Ilene Lelchuk, reporter at the *San Francisco Chronicle*, and Jim Staats, reporter at the *Marin Independent Journal*, thank you for finding this story and featuring it on your front pages, keeping the issue of bullying in the public eye. We commend you for being examples of the positive power of media. We are also grateful to Ryan White, reporter at the *Mill Valley Herald*, for your active interest in covering the community response to the project locally.

To Don Buder, thanks for being supportive of our idea for the "Olivia's Letters" project and for your editing input.

Finally, we want to thank the many thousands of compassionate people from all over the world who took time out of their busy lives to share their personal experiences and to convey support to Olivia. Every letter was an invaluable contribution to her progress.